ON FLOWERS

ON FLOWERS

LESSONS FROM AN ACCIDENTAL FLORIST

AMY MERRICK

ARTISAN | NEW YORK

Photographs on pages 28–29, 32–33, 72–73, 76–77, 79, 114–15, 158–59,
198–99, and 204–5 copyright © Tif Hunter; photograph on pages 46–47
copyright © F. Martin Ramin; photographs on pages 138–39, 142, 166, 170–71,
173, 177, 183, 207, 218, 219, 220–21, 223, 230, 231, 232–33,
234–35, and 236 copyright © Miyuki Yamakana.

Illustrations copyright © Giulia Garbin except page 130, *Cherry Blossom* by Ogawa Kazumasa,
printed with permission from the Rijksmuseum; page 131 by Lesley Blanch,
from *Hostess* by Constance Spry, published by J.M. Dent & Sons (1961) with permission
from The Orion Publishing Group; and page 169, *Gräser* by Fritz Kühn, printed with
permission from Achim Kühn, Berlin (Estate Collection FK).

Library of Congress Cataloging-in-Publication Data is on file.

ISBN 978-1-57965-812-0

Design by Giulia Garbin

Artisan books are available at special discounts when purchased in bulk for premiums and sales
promotions as well as for fund-raising or educational use. Special editions or book excerpts also
can be created to specification. For details, contact the Special Sales Director at the address below,
or send an e-mail to specialmarkets@workman.com.

For speaking engagements,
contact speakersbureau@workman.com.

Published by Artisan
A division of Workman Publishing Co., Inc.
225 Varick Street
New York, NY 10014-4381
artisanbooks.com

Artisan is a registered trademark of
Workman Publishing Co., Inc.

Published simultaneously in Canada by Thomas Allen & Son, Limited

Printed in China

First printing, September 2019

1 3 5 7 9 10 8 6 4 2

CONTENTS

Alas! th...
To be a...
For all of...
And if '...
bring
To them, but mockeries of the past alone.
BYRON.

July 5.

But if ye saw that which no eyes can see,
The inward beauty of her lively sp'rit,
Garnish'd with heavenly gifts of high de-
gree,
Much more would ye wonder at that sight,
And stand astonish'd, like to those which
r ad
Medusa's mazeful head.
There dwells sweet love and constant
chastity,
Unspotted faith, and comely womanhood,
Regard of honour, and mild modesty;
There Virtue reigns as queen on royal
throne,
And giveth laws alone,
The which the base affections do obey,
And yield their services unto her will.
SPENSER.

Mignonette—Excellence.

Iris—"I have a message for you."

July 6.

Go, blushing flower!
And tell her this from me,
That in the bower
From which I gathered thee,
At evening I will be.
PETER SPENCER.

MISS AMY ELIZABETH MERRICK

ELMWOOD
Hancock, New Hampshire

Dear readers,

On top of the old desk at my family's summerhouse, amid an assortment of dull pencils and letters and stacks of crisp white stationery embossed with ELMWOOD in emerald ink, there is a leather-bound volume called "The Floral Birthday Book." Published in 1876, it assigns each day of the year a flower, with an accompanying meaning, poem, and watercolor illustration alongside a small space to write names of loved ones. It is a treasure, with my ancestors' birth dates listed in a graceful, scrawling hand, and I'm sure it was the first flower book I ever read.

I've written "On Flowers," a floral book of my own, to celebrate all the ways to appreciate flowers—the fancy and the humble, the urban and the rural, and the faraway flowers I fell in love with on my travels. It was meant to be a book about flower arranging, but it grew into something more: a bouquet of memories and meditations meant to show you how to see flowers, rather than ways to simply put them in a vase.

Following this note is a little manual that distills the collected wisdom from my years as a floral designer in New York City and subsequent career teaching flower arranging all over the world. Then the real adventure starts, with each chapter presenting a new way of appreciating and arranging flowers, no matter where you find yourself.

In "The Floral Birthday Book," my birthday flower is a little blue iris, and its meaning is "I have a message for you." This very Victorian sentiment was always a great mystery to me as a girl; I was desperate to know who was going to give me the message, and what would it be. Only recently did I see my flower's meaning in a different light: it's you I have a message for, one I've waited my whole life to share. And I couldn't be more pleased that you're holding it now in your hands.

Yours truly,

Amy Merrick

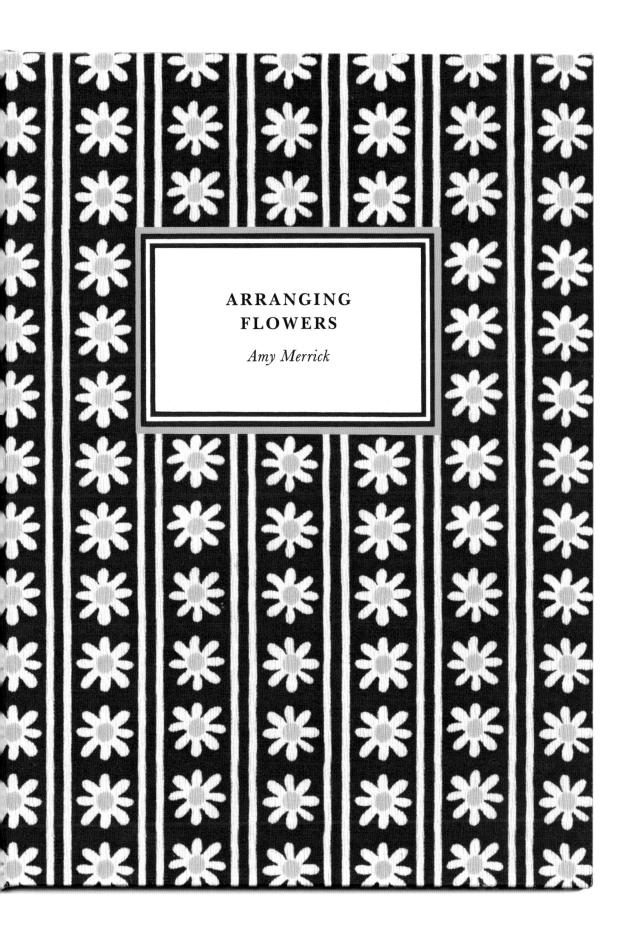

ARRANGING FLOWERS

Amy Merrick

HOW TO SELECT FLOWERS

C hoosing flowers is the most important part of making an arrangement. Once you've done that, the hardest work is already finished. Your pairing of colors and textures will set the mood for your creation and allow your own unique voice to shine. First, determine the spirit of your arrangement: maybe a subtle whisper with tiny trembling wildflowers, or perhaps a chorus of color and contrast with big bold blooms? Something architecturally sparse or dripping with romance? Next, select your flowers, using season, color, and texture to guide your choices and evoke your chosen mood. Flowers speak. What would you like them to say?

SEASON

To love flowers is to revere nature, and to revere nature is to honor seasons. This ethos should dictate your floral selections—anything else would feel boorish in these modern times. Seasonal flowers have an unmatched vitality and character, an of-the-moment insouciance that even the most opulent imported blooms lack. They offer crooked, whimsical stems; unique colors; nuanced variegation; and unusual varieties—they are often fresher and a better value, too. Seasons are different in every corner of the world, and your observations will inspire arrangements that feel truly of their place. Look outside your window and find something beautiful.

COLOR

Color is an enticement, a botanical come-hither whose spell is cast on pollinators and people alike. To impose my own palette preferences on your creativity would be stifling, and it would be useless, too; I'm hopelessly fickle, and any passing hue can catch my eye. (I must admit, however, I often worry about people who like only white flowers.) It is sufficient to say that on the color wheel, neighbors will harmonize and opposites will vibrate. Look to nature's own variegation for surprising combinations, and never stop experimenting with subtle shifts in hue and the feelings they evoke. It's worth noting that green acts as nature's neutralizer: a lot of green foliage will drain the drama from a vase of bright blooms.

TEXTURE

Velvety, creamy, glossy, feathery, papery, waxy, crinkly; tactile textures are sumptuous pleasures of nature. Contrasts in texture can add an element of surprise—think of the willowy grace of a vine cascading through the architecture of a thorny branch, or perhaps a pillowy pile of blooms studded with clusters of berries. Pairing similar textures can also be dramatic: a large, diaphanous bunch of lacy wildflowers gathered into billowing clouds, each wispy stem holding significantly more impact when used en masse. Texture adds a delightful depth to any arrangement.

HOW TO CHOOSE A VASE

Selecting a vase is an exercise in proportion, a conversation between the size and shape of your flowers and your container. There is a sixth sense when it comes to choosing the right-size vase, but luckily, it is a sense that can be improved through practice, similar to learning to taste hitherto undetectable flavors in expensive wine. The perfect flower in the perfect vase is a marriage of equals—color, proportion, and spirit in agreement.

Vase is a fluid word. Really, it can be anything that holds water: a salad bowl, an antique treasure, a coffee cup, a lovely piece of pottery, a rusty bucket, a tiny shell flipped upside down to make a miniature dish. Cherish vases and keep them clean; a spotless vase will aid in keeping bacteria at bay.

These are the shapes I love most: **BUD VASE** Find a single perfect flower, and the work is done for you. **FOOTED VASE** Elegant for refined, painterly arrangements. **SHALLOW BOWL** Float a few stems, or use additional support to create a full centerpiece in the round. **PITCHER** Lovely for effortless, natural wildflower bouquets. **GINGER JAR** A graceful, gently rounded body with a narrow mouth. Deliciously simple and stable. **MINIATURE VASE** A witty wink for a small stem.

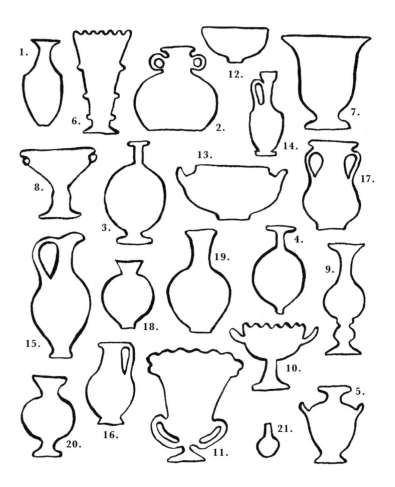

A few of my favorite vases

1.–5. BUD VASES 6.–11. FOOTED VASES 12.–13. SHALLOW BOWLS
14.–16. PITCHERS 17.–20. GINGER JARS 21. MINIATURE VASE

How to use a flower frog

FLOWER HOLDERS

Wide or shallow containers often require additional structural support to be used for flower arrangements. When stems cannot stand on their own, creating a base using one of the tools below will help things along.

NATURAL MATERIALS A small branch with stems tucked inside a vase makes a delightfully simple and effective internal support for opaque containers. The interlacing twigs will form a web to hold flowers in place; just be sure to remove all the leaves before you start.

FLOWER FROGS These wonders are best suited to shallow vases or bowls, and are most helpful for arrangements that will not need to be transported. The sharp pin variety is especially useful. Old frogs can be found for just a few dollars at flea markets and yard sales and are heavy enough to hold an arrangement on their own, but newly produced frogs need to be attached to a vessel's bottom with floral adhesive, available at craft stores. The following page shows my personal collection of flower frogs.

CHICKEN WIRE This is a user-friendly option for vases with wide mouths; when balled up, it makes for a very strong and reusable structure. Wire cutters are crucial here, as repeated wire snippings will ravage your floral clippers.

Please avoid floral foam, a rather distasteful petroleum-based material that does not biodegrade and gives arrangements an unnatural rigidity.

My flower frog collection

1.–4. PIN HOLDERS (OR *KENZAN*), USED TO PIERCE STEMS IN PLACE
5.–11. VINTAGE METAL CAGES   **12.–14.** CERAMIC DOMES WITH HOLES
FOR STEMS   **15.** A GLASS HOLDER, LOVELY WHEN VISIBLE IN A BOWL

*There are many different varieties of flower frogs to collect. The pin variety originated
in Japan, where it is called* kenzan–*in English, "sword mountain."*

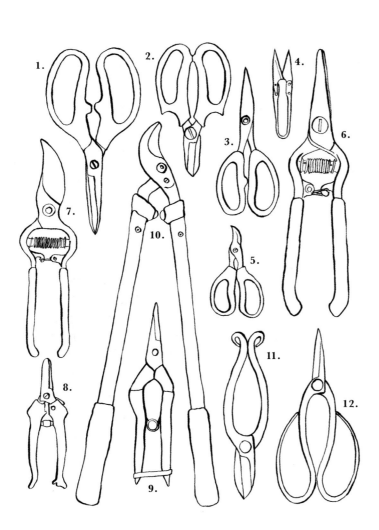

My clipper collection

1.–5. FLORAL SHEARS, FOR SOFT STEMS   6.–9. GARDEN SECATEURS, FOR WOODY OR THICK STEMS   10. LOPERS, FOR LARGE BRANCHES 11.–12. JAPANESE CLIPPERS, FOR SPECIAL OCCASIONS

You don't need fancy clippers. As long as you keep them clean and sharp, they will get the job done. My favorites are made for ikebana; they chime like a bell as you snip.

THE PROCESS OF ARRANGING

1.
PREPARATION
OF MATERIALS

2.
STRUCTURAL
FOUNDATION

3.
FOCAL
FLOWERS

4.
GESTURAL
FLOURISH

1. PREPARATION OF MATERIALS Choose a vase. Insert a frog or other supporting structure if needed. Fill the vase with water. Condition your flowers by removing any leaves that fall below the vase waterline, or that will detract from your arrangement.

2. STRUCTURAL FOUNDATION Use leaves, branches, or a substantial mass of flowers to build your overall shape. By starting with sturdy stems, you create a firm base to support more delicate flowers.

3. FOCAL FLOWERS These are the most eye-catching blooms. Try placing one directly on the edge of the vase for both visual and mechanical stability. By cutting them to different lengths, you add dimension and levels to an arrangement. Once you have placed the focal flowers, smaller supporting flowers can be used to fill out your vase.

4. GESTURAL FLOURISH For levity and movement, add something unexpected: a wisp of tall, feathery grass; a tendril of vines; or a pair of tiny blooms dancing above a display. This finishing touch is a perfect chance to make a final splash with scale, providing a sense of whimsy with delicate stems that would otherwise be overwhelmed in an arrangement.

PROPORTION AND SHAPE

Proportion and shape are essential design principles that will help you elevate an otherwise delightful arrangement to an art form.

PROPORTION This is your sense of scale, and also your sense of humor. Traditional floral wisdom states that elegant arrangements rest between one and a half and two and a half times the height of the vase. This principle is by no means a hard-and-fast rule, but I do rather like the absurdity of getting out the ruler when approaching something as spontaneous as flower arranging, and it's quite useful when a beginner reaches for a vase. Classical proportions can be learned, then promptly disregarded to make way for personal style.

SHAPE This captures your overall sense of balance and movement. An architecturally upright arrangement with a strong, balanced vertical appears to grow toward the sun. An asymmetrical form with a dynamic, offset movement could evoke flowers caught up in the breeze. Maybe your arrangement is in a footed vase with no vertical note at all, cascading dramatically, like a waterfall flowing from rock to rock.

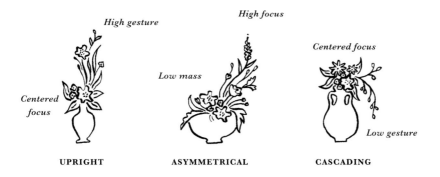

High gesture

High focus

Centered focus

Low mass

Centered focus

Low gesture

UPRIGHT   **ASYMMETRICAL**   **CASCADING**

THE STORY OF AN ARRANGEMENT

Now I'll show you how an arrangement is born, both in concept and creation. This is your chance to peek behind the curtain to see my process. These otherwise simple flowers become extraordinary when combined thoughtfully. (And I do hope you notice the bug-chewed holes.)

1. I love this little black GINGER JAR for its graceful, petite proportions and narrow opening; it is a vase I reach for often.

2. The yellow LEAVES had fallen from a tree; their charming, graphic shape reminded me of Matisse paper cutouts. They were long stemmed, so I decided to use them as a foundation.

3. A single fuchsia CAMELLIA, complete with a juicy bud, caught my eye; its vibrant pink bounced when I placed it next to the bright yellow leaves. This became my focal flower and went just on the lip of my vase, creating a low focal point to balance an asymmetrical silhouette. I left the burgundy leaves, but I would have removed them if they were green— they would have subdued the dramatic palette.

4. Two small stems of pink CHRYSANTHEMUM provided sweetness and some much-needed textural detail as supporting flowers.

5. For a grand finale, a delicate and snappy THIN BRANCH added a charming gestural flourish; a strong, lithe line to lighten an otherwise heavy composition. While the twig feels insubstantial on its own, in this combination it is the exclamation point at the end of a vibrant autumnal sentence.

A walk in the park

PRACTICAL POINTS FOR
FLOWER CARE

1. Keep vases and clippers scrupulously clean.

2. Whether flowers are plucked from the garden or bought at a shop, trim their stems at a 45-degree angle immediately before placing them in water.

3. To extend the life of your flowers, allow them to hydrate in water for an hour or more before arranging.

4. To hurry closed buds such as peonies or lilies into bloom, give them a long drink of warm water.

5. Flowers that have wilted on the journey home can be revived; gently wrap them in paper, and place them in a shady corner.

6. Vases should always be filled to the very top with room-temperature water. There is nothing more stingy than offering flowers a paltry few inches to drink.

7. Below the vase waterline is a sacred space: no leaves are allowed. They will rot and feed bacteria that turn vase water into an unpleasant swamp that will shorten a flower's life.

8. Refresh vase water daily. This is a better option than flower food, that noxious chemical nonsense best avoided in homes.

9. Arrangements should be kept in cooler corners, out of direct sun, for the longest life.

10. Vase life varies dramatically from flower to flower. Bear fleeting blooms no ill-will; learn to appreciate this part of their charm.

SPECIAL TRICKS FOR FUSSY FLOWERS

CHRYSANTHEMUMS

Mums do not like metal clippers. Break their stems to the desired length by hand.

WOODY BRANCHES

Crush or break branches upward perpendicularly to allow for more water flow.

ROSES

To prolong the life of delicate garden varieties, submerge their stems in water and recut. Warm water will help to open rosebuds.

DAFFODILS

Just-cut daffodils ooze a sticky sap that shortens the life of other stems in a vase. Before using, give them an hour in water alone.

TULIPS

If freshly bought tulips appear floppy, wrap them in paper for support, then place them upright in a vase or bucket of water to hydrate for an hour.

POPPIES

Sear poppy stems by dipping the bottom inch in boiling water; this cauterization aids hydration. Peel open any reluctant buds after a day or two.

To see a world in a grain of sand,
And a heaven in a wild flower,
Hold infinity in the palm of your hand,
And eternity in an hour.

—William Blake

IN

CI

THE
TY

New York City gave me flowers. Most people think of cities as barren concrete wastelands, but without those sidewalks, I never would have found my botanical path. My own urban awakening is a common enough story: young woman seeks divine enlightenment through culture, creativity, and a career in fashion. After a few years of high heels, parties, and destroyed dry-clean-only dresses, I discovered that maybe I didn't have the constitution for the fashion rat race, even if I did love the uniform. I left my plush job to venture into the unknown, cobbling together a living through freelance prop styling and the occasional writing assignment.

In those first few years of city life, I began to ache for the green I'd grown up with in the countryside and started to seek out traces of nature wherever I went. And when I started to look—and I mean passionately and single-mindedly look—I discovered that even in the city, I didn't have to look far at all. On every city block, birds nested, geraniums spilled from window boxes, and wildflowers pushed up from cracks in the sidewalk. And that doesn't even take into account the vast botanical gardens, classically refined parks, and sunny marble courtyards all over town. Hotel lobbies burst forth with towering flower arrangements, museums exhibited priceless painted bouquets, and even pigeon-pecked corner stores flooded the streets with buckets of blooms, creating a cellophane-swathed garden that changed as surely as the weather. For city dwellers, the earliest seasonal harbingers often come at five dollars a pop.

With my newfound flexibility, I visited the Brooklyn Botanic Garden every Tuesday, when admission was free. I'd sneak into the branches of the weeping beech tree, just off the bluebell wood, turning to its familiar green canopy for refuge. There I plotted to take a flower-arranging class just for fun, and during that search, I found a flower shop looking for a one-day-a-week intern—a position paid in flowers. Ever the pragmatist, I thought it seemed like a good bargain; rather than spend money on a class, I could walk away with armfuls of flowers. Instinct and opportunity combined in a single spark, an innate moment of full-body yes. Life as a florist seamlessly combined my inclination for nature with my stylistic pursuits. Within a year, my third-floor apartment had become a floral studio, with a bathtub full of branches and a bed strewn with stems, and the rest is history. My longing for flowers, and my life working with them, sprung from the sidewalk.

AMY MERRICK
FLOWERS

SIDEWALK FLOWER STANDS

NATO BROS.

LOOKING AT DOWNTOWN SKYLINE FROM UNDER BROOKLYN BRIDGE, NEW YORK CITY

HERE IS NEW YORK

E. B. WHITE

Author of "One Man's Meat"

MTA MetroC

Insert this way / This

An iconic New York City coffee cup, full to the brim with liquid gold: daffodils, narcissus, and chamomile.

FINDING

FLOWER MARKETS

Flower markets offer an impressive array of local and imported flowers available in bulk year-round. If your city has a wholesale market, inquire about daily passes for visitors or specific hours for the public. Bring cash and ask questions: prices, provenance, and flower care are good places to start. Go early, go often, and learn something.

FARMERS' MARKETS

Painterly piles of beautiful fruits and vegetables in every color imaginable, alongside buckets of seasonal flowers; farmers' markets are the best place to scoop up inspiration and ingredients. I often buy produce to combine with flowers. Nothing is more gorgeous on your kitchen table than that bounty, effortlessly displayed.

GROCERY STORES

Fancy grocery stores often have a serviceable floral section with a mix of local bunches and simple potted plants. For the same price as a bouquet, a potted flowering plant will have weeks' worth of blooms; swap out the plastic pot for mossy terracotta, and enjoy.

FLOWER SHOPS

A good florist creates an enchanting portal in the city, an entire world of magical flowers just off the street. Florists can make jaw-dropping arrangements, but I often buy loose stems to arrange at home. Sometimes I get just one perfect flower; there is no better way to spend bus fare.

How does one love, cherish, and find flowers in city?

FLOWERS

CORNER STORES

Cheap and colorful bunches spill down the sidewalk; it's so easy to grab one alongside your Sunday morning newspaper. Ask for what's in season and always check for freshness. Vibrant leaves, firm petals, and recently cut stems are good indicators.

PARKS

Picking flowers from public parks and street gardens makes you a thoughtless neighbor. It might seem tempting, but nothing breaks my heart more than broken stems from someone's careless foraging. Make friends with the landscapers, though; they are the source of many wonderful trimmings that would otherwise be tossed.

ALLEYS AND CRACKS

Use your highly developed moral compass to determine if the object of your affection was planted or is being tended or enjoyed. If so, don't cut it! If it seems truly neglected and unwanted, proceed with gentleness, caution, and clippers. It should look as though you were never there.

PARKING LOTS

Before picking flowers from lots, ask the lots' owners, with homemade cookies in hand for added persuasive power. I've made many interesting neighborhood friends this way, and they often are surprised and thrilled to help. No one has refused my many foraging forays so far.

IN YOUR OWN POT

Consider joining a community garden to grow your own flowers, or splurge on beautiful window boxes to fill with annuals for the occasional snip. I turned my third-floor fire escape into a veritable jungle, with sweet peas climbing the ladder and pots spilling over with herbs.

There are many avenues and alleys to take.

HOW TO MAKE CHEAP FLOWERS LOOK EXPENSIVE

1.

Banish cellophane. Instead, choose a decorative paper to match the mood of your flowers.

2.

Remove any rubber bands and separate stems. Recut each stem to a slightly different height. (This is the most useful tip for beginners in the whole book.)

3.

Crisply fold an oblong rectangle of your chosen paper in half, so it's roughly three-quarters the height of your bunch.

4.

Place your flowers so that they are roughly level with the top of the paper and the stems are exposed at the bottom.

5.

Grasping the paper and stems with one hand, roll so that the paper wraps the bouquet, using your other hand to stabilize it.

6.

Tie the wrapped bouquet tightly with a pretty ribbon or bit of fancy string, in the backseat of a taxicab on your way to a dinner party. (The best guests show up at the front door with their arms overflowing.)

Opposite: Grabbing a taxi to head downtown? Some mini carnations, daisies, baby's breath, and Queen Anne's lace, all wrapped up in the *New York Times*, ought to do the trick.

A VASE OF GROCERY-STORE FLOWERS LOOKING RATHER
CHIC IN A 1950S, ALMOST PAINTED SORT OF WAY.

While this all looks very civilized, I actually arranged it in the park, surrounded by pigeons, on my way home from the store. Starring here are carnations of different sizes and red and coral gladiolus, crowned by two irises for drama. I debated adding the irises, but without them, the arrangement would have veered into monotony. I used to look down on gladiolus (too banal, I thought), but every day a new flower opens, and what could be more cheerful?

SAY IT WITH FLOWERS One day I want
to write a screenplay for a classic romantic comedy in the
manner of *You've Got Mail*. A single florist spends her days
in New York City arranging flowers for weddings, writing
out other people's love notes, and learning the deepest inner
workings of the relationships in her neighborhood. There is
no better primer in the realm of romance than the local flower
shop; our florist leading lady is truly the gatekeeper of love.
There are endless possible plotlines: the customer who buys
flowers for both his wife and his girlfriend. The woman who
sends herself an arrangement from a so-called secret admirer.
The florist's own ex-boyfriend who has the audacity to order
a Valentine's Day bouquet for his current girlfriend. (I will
own that this screenplay is completely autobiographical and
that any resemblance to ex-boyfriends, living or ought-to-be
dead, is 100 percent intentional.)

Now, our heroine has never been sent a bouquet herself, for it is an unwritten law of the universe that no one
ever sends a florist flowers. She has always wondered what it
would be like to see the deliveryman at the door, to feel that
flush of pleasure—smelling the bouquet, opening the little
card, flooded with curiosity about the sender. This is a ritual
our heroine may never know; it is one of the great mysteries
of a florist's life. I haven't worked out the ending yet. Maybe
our florist finds someone brave enough to send her a bouquet
and thoughtful enough to know that even something simple
will do. In the meantime, I will continue to send flowers as
research, little dispatches of admiration to all those I love.

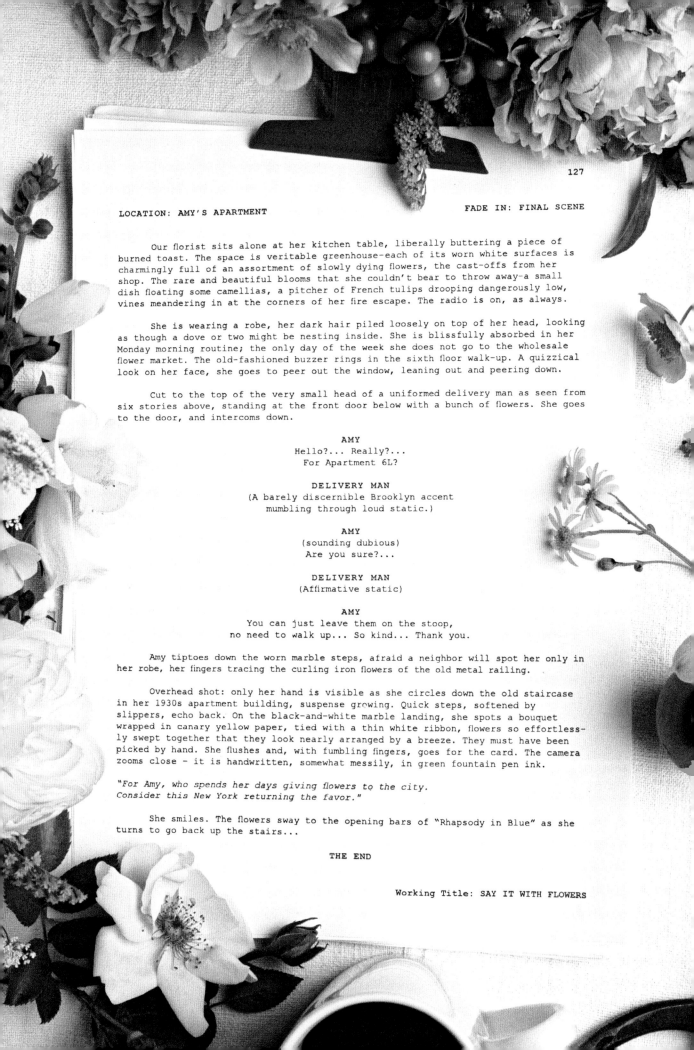

LOCATION: AMY'S APARTMENT   FADE IN: FINAL SCENE

Our florist sits alone at her kitchen table, liberally buttering a piece of burned toast. The space is veritable greenhouse-each of its worn white surfaces is charmingly full of an assortment of slowly dying flowers, the cast-offs from her shop. The rare and beautiful blooms that she couldn't bear to throw away-a small dish floating some camellias, a pitcher of French tulips drooping dangerously low, vines meandering in at the corners of her fire escape. The radio is on, as always.

She is wearing a robe, her dark hair piled loosely on top of her head, looking as though a dove or two might be nesting inside. She is blissfully absorbed in her Monday morning routine; the only day of the week she does not go to the wholesale flower market. The old-fashioned buzzer rings in the sixth floor walk-up. A quizzical look on her face, she goes to peer out the window, leaning out and peering down.

Cut to the top of the very small head of a uniformed delivery man as seen from six stories above, standing at the front door below with a bunch of flowers. She goes to the door, and intercoms down.

AMY
Hello?... Really?...
For Apartment 6L?

DELIVERY MAN
(A barely discernible Brooklyn accent
mumbling through loud static.)

AMY
(sounding dubious)
Are you sure?...

DELIVERY MAN
(Affirmative static)

AMY
You can just leave them on the stoop,
no need to walk up... So kind... Thank you.

Amy tiptoes down the worn marble steps, afraid a neighbor will spot her only in her robe, her fingers tracing the curling iron flowers of the old metal railing.

Overhead shot: only her hand is visible as she circles down the old staircase in her 1930s apartment building, suspense growing. Quick steps, softened by slippers, echo back. On the black-and-white marble landing, she spots a bouquet wrapped in canary yellow paper, tied with a thin white ribbon, flowers so effortlessly swept together that they look nearly arranged by a breeze. They must have been picked by hand. She flushes and, with fumbling fingers, goes for the card. The camera zooms close - it is handwritten, somewhat messily, in green fountain pen ink.

*"For Amy, who spends her days giving flowers to the city.
Consider this New York returning the favor."*

She smiles. The flowers sway to the opening bars of "Rhapsody in Blue" as she turns to go back up the stairs...

THE END

Working Title: SAY IT WITH FLOWERS

HOW TO SEND FLOWERS
LIKE A FLORIST

I.

Find a local shop you trust.

2.

When options are limited, any florist should
be able to put together a big mass of a single,
seasonal variety—a much chicer choice than
a dubious mixed bouquet.

3.

Inquire a week in advance, be open about your
budget, and ask about delivery fees.

4.

If you order from a great flower shop, let them
take the lead in terms of variety. They know what
will be the most beautiful that day.

5.

Feel free to make suggestions about color or mood
depending on personality and occasion.

6.

If you have an especially personal message to include,
send your own note ahead of time. Some things
should really be said in your own handwriting.

Opposite: Often, a single flower you've picked yourself is the nicest bouquet you can give.

When you take a flower in your hand and
really look at it, it's your world for
the moment. I want to give that world
to someone else. Most people in the
city rush around so, they have no time
to look at a flower. I want them to see
it whether they want to or not.

—Georgia O'Keeffe

Sometimes you have to stick your neck
out to thrive in a city.

A single stem of celosia, growing through a
crack in the cement. Someone taped it
up to keep it from flopping into the street.

WILD THINGS There is an abandoned, over-grown parking lot in Brooklyn where the most wonderful things appear—tufts of wild lilac asters, tall milkweed pods just about to burst, little robin's-egg-blue porcelain vines twisting through the chain-link fence, Queen Anne's lace peeking up through the cracks. I'd long lusted to do some snipping behind the fence but never felt brave enough to ask. Instead, I'd simply make a point of walking a full three blocks out of my way to stare wistfully at this parking-lot paradise—a repeated reconnaissance mission for a siege I would one day make.

Life, though, is too short to let fear, or fences, hold you back, so eventually I worked up the courage and knocked on the front door of the municipal office with the only access to the overgrown lot. Would they let me cut some things for a party I was having that night? I got puzzled looks and shrugs of permission, and when the janitor led me into the lot, he stuck around, finding treasures of his own. We clipped together, both beaming with delight at each small discovery. I left with enough wild and weedy bounty for a few bouquets, plucked with permission from the best secret flower shop in town.

Opposite: Wild poppies, growing through asphalt.

Goldenrod, rose hips, asters, clematis seed heads, and rudbeckia foraged from the forgotten corners of Brooklyn in late October.

An aster from the street. I couldn't help but pick the ginkgo leaf, too. They belong together.

"Say it with Flowers"

Guest Check

TABLE NO.	PERSONS	WAITER	CHECK NO.
			977502

PORTIONS		AMOUNT
	primroses from the market	$3
	daisies from the alleyway	free
	peonies and poppies from the florist	$5/each
	matching your flowers to your breakfast	priceless
	TAX	

HOW TO BE A
GRACIOUS FORAGER

I.

Always ask permission.

2.

Respect areas off-limits for foraging: public parks,
front gardens, planters, window boxes,
sidewalk tree beds, and planted road medians.

3.

Use clippers. Don't rip stems or pull plants;
leave a space looking as though nothing has
been cut at all.

4.

Take only what you genuinely will use
(it's often less than you imagine).

5.

Be gentle and restrained. It would be heartbreaking
if all the spry little volunteers that give city streets
so much character were snipped.

Opposite: Good city citizens, drawn by William Steig for *The New Yorker*.

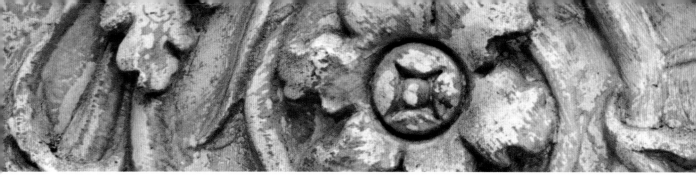

A MARBLE GARDEN

It's an old habit I have, taking myself on a solo date to a museum to see flowers. I've formed long-standing love affairs with certain paintings, and these have outlasted many real-life romances. A lovely dress and some decent shoes are mandatory on these afternoons; it's important to make an effort when the object of your affection is so elegant. The swish of leather soles on a marble museum floor is, without a doubt, one of my favorite metropolitan sounds—the big-city equivalent of hopping from stone to stone across a little running stream.

I can easily remember those same steps from a childhood spent haunting the Smithsonian museums in Washington, DC, just an hour's drive from my family's farmhouse on the Chesapeake Bay. My mother floated, floral skirt billowing behind her, along those museum hallways with my sister and me trailing behind. When the weather was steamy, we went for education and air-conditioning; in the winter, paintings bloomed for us when all else was bare. Together, we traveled with the fervor of explorers through every museum within reach. We shopped with our eyes, amassing incredible private art collections, each picking a piece on

our way out the door when my mother asked, "Okay, girls, what will you choose today?"

Thanks to her, I still waltz over museum floors, gathering my favorites. Pale lavender paired with tangerine floats to the surface of an otherwise placid Monet water lily; I would have never imagined those colors could be so delightful together until he showed me. An oversized, dreamlike tropical bouquet peeks out from behind a leaf in a Rousseau jungle and I'm transported to the Amazon, aching to arrange wild orchids and dramatic, juicy green leaves. A Matisse kitchen table practically sets itself with sunny ceramics and textiles—bright flowers, stripes, fruit, and me, leaning over the table in an Edwardian kimono, pouring coffee in the sunshine. Painted flowers hold the most meaning when we spring them from their gilded frames and into our own worlds, onto our own tables.

This floral reverie became reality when a cherished fashion client called; she was hosting a party at the Metropolitan Museum of Art to celebrate the opening of *Punk: Chaos to Couture*, an exhibition held by the Costume Institute. The sanctified European Sculpture Court was to be splashed and slashed in honor of the party, and

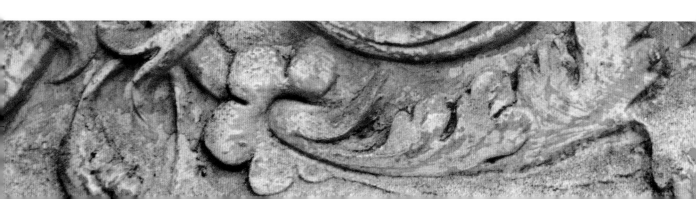

it was my job to dream up the subversive flowers to follow suit. What could be more punk than dead flowers? A picturesque English garden gone feral—a snarled, savage world of feminine beauty, Miss Havisham by way of Vivienne Westwood. The roots of classic romanticism neglected, a thicket of thorns poised to entangle, petals pooling and vines choking candelabras tarnished with heavy drips of black wax.

It was early May, so peonies were in their prime, and the first of the velvety roses were flushing. It was a laugh to explain to the client that dead flowers cost no less than fresh ones, as the only way to have dead flowers is to buy them and let time cast its spell. I made the bouquets in advance, and an early heat wave helped them wilt, but eventually I just poured the water out of the vases for maximum decay. The van ride to the museum was a terror—I was petrified that the peonies would explode, that the roses would disintegrate, that I would have only stems, no meat left on the bone. As my team and I crawled our way into the bowels of the museum, through the secret basement service entrance, the magic of it all overtook me. My work—my dead, divine flowers—decorating the hallowed halls of the museum. Pools of bloodred peony petals fell to the tables, black velvet roses clawed and kissed the tattered tablecloths, a briar of vines entwined themselves through the wax-dripped candelabras. Flowers and vines tied in a knot, a disarrangement of romantic decay. From a black garbage bag I brought from home emerged the crowning glory: a tangle of English ivy foraged off the chain-link fence in the alley behind my apartment. Grime from the Brooklyn street still clung to its tough stem, covered with hairy clinging suckers so like the legs of an oversized centipede. This unidentifiable dirt gracing the tables of the highest of New York society was my own little punk moment. Who knows what else might have coated those leaves?

As night fell and the black candles were lit, we slipped out of the party, sneaking through the empty halls of the Grecian wing, a gang of floral outlaws. We spilled out the front doors, down the cold gray granite steps onto the corner of Eighty-Second Street, just as the sun was setting over Central Park. Back onto the streets, into blue night air, with cabs whizzing down Fifth Avenue, streetlights glowing: one enchanted evening in a marble garden.

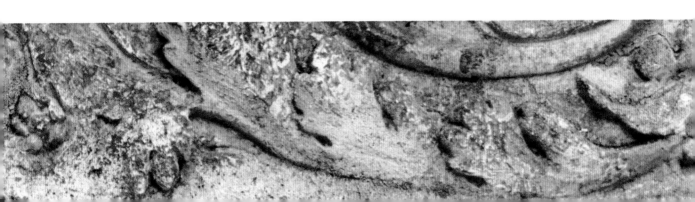

I brought a print of Pierre Bonnard's *The Studio with Mimosa* to the flower market and picked flowers to match: Icelandic poppies, fritillaria, and butterfly ranunculus.

MUSEUMS

FLOWER LOVERS

GLASS FLOWERS
HARVARD MUSEUM OF NATURAL HISTORY
Cambridge, Massachusetts, USA

This original Victorian gallery boasts an achingly beautiful collection of nearly a thousand lifelike nineteenth-century floral specimens, created in hand-blown glass by Leopold and Rudolf Blaschka as botanical models for study.

THE GARDEN MUSEUM
London, UK

Boasting an unmatched collection of antique garden tools, paintings, and floral ephemera, London's Garden Museum is a hub of British horticulture, both past and present. Wander in the lofty galleries and soak up some quiet in the Dan Pearson–designed courtyard garden, which contains the tomb of famed sixteenth-century naturalist John Tradescant.

ISABELLA STEWART GARDNER MUSEUM
Boston, Massachusetts, USA

An enchanting art museum and courtyard garden disguised as the most exquisite life-size dollhouse, complete with singing canaries to provide a natural sound track. The entrancing nasturtiums in the courtyard are world famous—they trail down from the balcony, over twenty feet long.

MARIANNE NORTH GALLERY AT KEW
Richmond, Surrey, UK

This eye-popping gallery displays richly painted tropical flower portraits captured in their native landscapes by the intrepid Victorian traveler and botanical artist Marianne North. Every inch of wall space is covered with the floral souvenirs from her worldwide adventures.

MERTZ LIBRARY ART GALLERY
NEW YORK BOTANICAL GARDEN
Bronx, New York, USA

The New York Botanical Garden's vast collection of botanical art and herbarium specimens is a destination for the horticulturally prepossessed. The gallery hosts rotating exhibitions, such as Charles Darwin's nature notebooks or Georgia O'Keeffe's paintings.

NAMIKAWA CLOISONNÉ MUSEUM
Kyoto, Japan

A tiny museum for tiny flowers, this house museum is the workshop, home, and garden of nineteenth-century cloisonné artist Namikawa Yasuyuki, famous for his delicate miniature enameled vases covered in flowers, every petal individually outlined in scrolled wire, each no larger than the point of a pencil.

NEUE GALERIE
New York, New York, USA

This jewel box of a museum is perhaps the most elegantly proportioned and presented in the world. Come for the superlative collection of Austrian and German art, but linger over the sublime lobby flower arrangements. Cozying up with Viennese coffee and cake at Café Sabarsky is my favorite city date.

NEZU MUSEUM
Tokyo, Japan

The official gem in this glossy museum is a certified National Treasure of Japan—Ogata Kōrin's seventeenth-century paneled folding screen depicting irises floating in a pond of golden lacquer. After your visit, wander the paths of the garden outside to see pools of iris and sip a matcha in the teahouse.

A lady on the street.

A lady at home.

Above: A stem of hydrangea with a dusty branch of foraged privet berries for a base and lavender clematis bought from a florist. But what would this arrangement be without the drip of a passion vine and that lace flower crown?

Opposite: Queen Anne's lace, pressed between the pages of a book.

WHEN

PLACED

IN A

SMALL

VASE,

A

SINGLE

WHITE

CYCLAMEN

IS

A

POEM

WITH

WINGS.

To be a wildflower growing in a meadow must feel a lot like living in a city.
Neighboring plants pressing close, ceaseless buzzing bees, everyone elbowing for
the same space. Competition is fierce, and privacy is nonexistent; life in meadows
must be very metropolitan indeed. But out of that chaos grows community—roots
and stems intertwine to allow movement without collapse. If you were a wildflower
billowing in the breeze, a city street might feel a lot like home.

CITY THINGS TO DO

Look both ways before crossing the street to look at flowers.

Stay on the grass.

Start an imaginary art collection.

Walk the long way, preferably through the park.

Put bouquets in your window.

Smile when you see flowers in someone else's window.

Watch birds in the park.

Throw a picnic dinner party.

Carry flowers on the subway.

Order dinner at midnight, because you can.

Talk to taxi drivers.

Walk in all kinds of weather.

Go to the botanical garden in winter.

Overtip often.

Volunteer in a community garden.

Keep herbs on your windowsill.

Take yourself on a very fancy cake date.

Read a book on the train.

Make a container garden.

Know your local florist by name.

Say it with flowers.

IN

THE

COUNTRY

The truth of the matter is that I'm a country mouse, unrepentantly rural, even in my New York City days.

While you can take a girl out of the country and enchant her with metropolitan delights, it's harder to take an innate preference for patchwork quilts, freshly baked pies, and fistfuls of wildflowers out of the girl. As a devoted city florist, I'd arrive to magazine photo shoots with my flowers tucked into wicker baskets, a bucolic breeze blowing down the sidewalk. And while the city gave me flowers, it was the countryside that taught me to love them from the start.

There is no surer way to fall in love with the country than to wander through a gently overgrown garden barefoot at dawn, blades of grass collecting between your toes, or to run your hands along the tops of tall grass while walking in a meadow with a straw sun hat shading your neck. Picking buckets of blooms from a flower farm, bunching up wispy, wild bouquets along the way, is a purely country delight. So is setting a long table under a tree and eating dinner outside every night you can. My natural longing always leads me back to my family's old rambling summerhouse in rural New Hampshire. That landscape is at the heart of my connection to flowers.

After many years working as a florist in the city, I needed to dig deeper into my own understanding of nature, an understanding that seemed to flourish only when I spent time outside. I had experienced flowers as a source of creative expression and commercial success, but I knew that there was another level of intimacy that could come only from sinking my hands into the soil. My good friend and right-hand floral assistant Siri invited me to visit her family's flower farm for a week, a trip that changed the course of my life.

The farm, off the coast of Washington State on a tiny island, is a true back-to-the-land affair—all meals were cooked on a woodstove; all baths were taken outside under the stars. The flowers were beyond compare, and Siri's family's warmth and generosity were complete. I decided to pause the floral career I had strived so hard to establish to work alongside them on the farm, refilling my own vase with fresh water in the process. I returned to the country to fall back in love with flowers, but I found that the country made me fall in love with my own life again.

U-PICK FLOWERS
ARE
READY

All *Flowering Plants*
NEED TO BE
WATERED DAILY
‖ IF VERY DRY SUBMERGE THE ‖
POT IN WATER FOR TEN MINUTES ‖

CUT
FLOWERS

BY

THE PEA FAMILY
(Leguminosae)

WILD
Gorse, Vetches,
Clover, Trefoils

ORNAMENTAL
Sweet Pea, Lupin
Laburnum

Garden
Sca

Not all country flowers grow in the garden. These I made from tissue paper, inspired by Livia Cetti's *The Exquisite Book of Paper Flowers*.

EDIBLE

BORAGE

Sweet and star-like in blue or white, this herb's flowers are mild in flavor and can be eaten whole. They look especially pretty on iced baked goods.

CALENDULA

Calendula's soft and buttery petals are the perfect floral edible—they have minimal flavor but maximum decorative impact.

CARNATIONS

The spicy clove-scented petals of carnations can be separated and used to accent a dressed salad.

CHAMOMILE

Fresh chamomile flowers steeped in just-below-boiling water make a tea to tame any pre-bedtime anxieties.

CHIVE BLOSSOMS

The purple herbal flowers of chives are perfect on salads and in any savory dish where a subtle, allium crunch would be welcome. The flowers make a beautiful pink vinegar when steeped.

CHRYSANTHEMUMS

In Japanese cuisine, both mum petals and leaves are used to add an herbal flourish to vegetables and salads.

CORNFLOWERS

Delicate blue, purple, or white cornflower florets can be separated and sprinkled on sweet and savory plates alike thanks to their gentle flavor.

DAYLILIES

Akin in size and flavor to a squash blossom, daylily petals can be eaten whole in a salad, or stuffed with ricotta and gently panfried.

If you give a small child a flower, they'll usually try to eat it.

FLOWERS

DIANTHUS

As the carnation's small and gentle sister, dianthus boast petals that can be separated and used to bedeck sweets and savories.

GERANIUMS

Geranium petals can adorn salads, sweets, and savories, while scented geranium oil adds an elegant note to baked goods.

ŒILLET DES FLEURISTES
Double, nain, hatif, varié

LAVENDER

A distinctively flavorful herb, lavender (both blossom and essential oil) is often baked into sweets and swirled into drinks.

LILACS

The subtle floral fragrance of lilac is preserved when individual florets are crystalized in sugar and used on top of treats.

PENSÉE GÉANTE DE
ROGGLI MÉLANGE I⁰ CHOIX

MARIGOLDS

A single petal packs a surprisingly strong, herbal punch, so marigolds are best used for savory dishes.

NASTURTIUMS

Nasturtiums are a peppery and delicious addition to salads when used whole, and nasturtium leaves also supply a beautiful texture and soft bite to a leafy mix.

VIOLA CORNUTA

PANSIES

Pansies' large petals make a great focal splash in sweet or savory presentations, and they press beautifully into shortbread cookies.

ROSES

Candied rose petals, sparkling with sugar, are a romantic addition to any dessert. Rose water is also a classic ingredient in Middle Eastern sweets.

ŒILLET DE POÉTE
ROUGE ÉCLATANT

SUNFLOWERS

The large yellow petals of sunflowers are a summery addition to any leafy salad; their subtle nutty taste is reminiscent of their seeds.

VIOLETS

Edible in their entirety, violets are charming when sprinkled on salads and can be crystalized in sugar to bedeck confections.

I totally understand the impulse: the most beautiful things always seem edible.

A BIRTHDAY CAKE

My mother baked me a cake
the very same day I was
born: a cake for my zero
birthday. I was in a rush
to arrive; the whole thing
was over so fast she never
made it to the hospital.
With a brand-new little
baby in a Moses basket on
the kitchen counter, she
broke the eggs, stirred
the batter, and smoothed
the frosting without a
second thought. Some friends
and family came over that
night for an impromptu party
on the first day of my life.
(That cake was carrot, and I
was just a crumb.)

Opposite: Everyone deserves a homemade birthday cake. My friend Claire Ptak from Violet Cakes baked
this for me, and I covered it with flower confetti: pansies, crab-apple blossoms, and roses.

IN PRAISE OF PICKING There is a subtle but distinct difference between flowers you've picked yourself and those in a store-bought bunch. Floral philistines might not notice, but the rest of us can see a certain genuine naturalness that sweeps through handpicked flowers like a breeze. It is a country art, picking flowers, and one I practice often; an early-morning waltz outside, clippers in hand, dew underfoot, in pajamas, with a cup of coffee steaming. There is no better way to fill a vase than to step outside into your own yard, looking to see what's new. (And every day, there is something new.)

For buckets of blooms, pick-your-own farms grow rows of flowers waiting for a self-serve snip; the stems are sold by the pound, just like produce. Nurseries sell blooming plants for your garden, but I often buy them just to cut; it's cheaper than a premixed bouquet, and I can clip a few stems of scented geranium or begonias as I need them. For the wild at heart, even a few wisps of grass gathered from a bucolic corner will speak volumes in a vase. My clippers are always in my pocket in the country.

Handpicked flowers are like homemade cakes—much more appealing than store-bought. Off-kilter kinks, bug-bitten leaves, the surprising addition of wild unpurchasables that are inherently seasonal—the rural arranger just uses what's at hand. Country bouquets grow like gardens themselves, spirited and spontaneous, capturing the heart of a place and a moment in time.

Opposite: A little celadon vase from a yard sale, filled with all manner of cheerful wildflowers whose verticality adds polish and wit to an otherwise sweet bouquet.

HOW TO
PICK FLOWERS

1.

Pick your stems early in the morning
or evening, safe from hot afternoon sun.

2.

Bring a bucket or jar of cool water outside with
you, and submerge stems immediately after cutting.

3.

Varieties that have just one flower per stem,
such as sunflowers, zinnias, and dahlias,
should be picked when they're in full bloom
since they won't open in a vase after being cut.

4.

Varieties that have clusters of buds per stem, such as lilies,
asters, and delphiniums, can be picked while they're still
opening, as their show will continue in a vase.

5.

It's best to cut flowering plants just above a leaf
node, the place where a leaf joins a stem. This avoids
an unsightly stump and encourages new growth.

6.

Cut a variety of stem lengths, and you'll be
halfway done achieving a natural arrangement.

Opposite: A prism of edible flowers, freshly picked from the garden.

Farm jumble: foxgloves, marigolds, a poppy, carnations, and a big artichoke leaf.

Page 309

W. Saxifrage

Scabious

Meadow Saxifrage

A found postcard of dahlia farmer Alvin Todd taken by Kenneth Rogers.

Illustrations by Culpeper.

Color inspiration from a butterfly bookplate.

AT FIRST GLANCE, SUNFLOWERS HAVE NO SECRETS.

They're uncomplicated, radiant with happiness—countryish to a fault. Sometimes they're too rustic for elegant company, but the more unique varieties, with seeds ripening for the birds, look sprung from a canvas. Their faces hold a trace of sunlight, as they always turn their gaze toward the sky. I like to keep them rather upright, since that is how they grow, and mix shapes and sizes, in various stages of bud, bloom, and seed. Van Gogh must have known this secret, too.

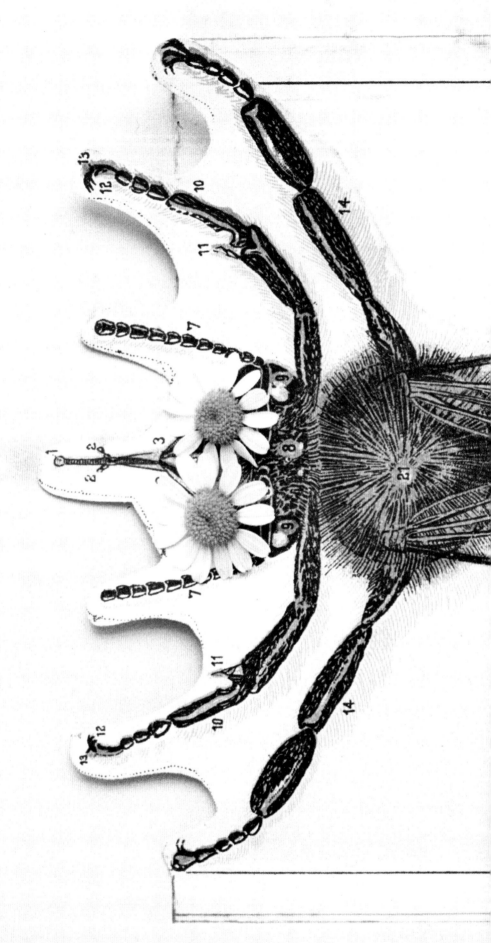

A bee from *The Nature Book*, published by Cassell & Co. in 1908.

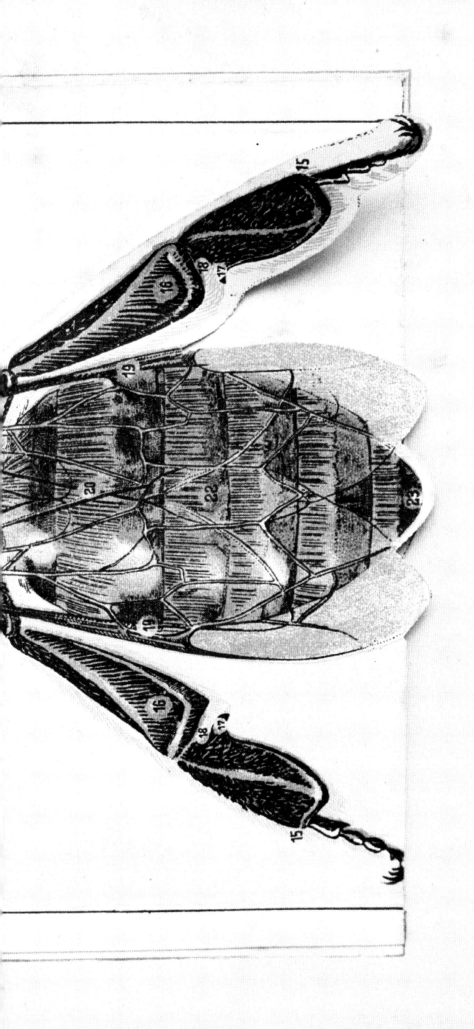

Above: 'Double Click' cosmos from Siri's flower farm.

Opposite: Speckled foxgloves and ruffled cosmos, arranged with a flower frog in a bowl.

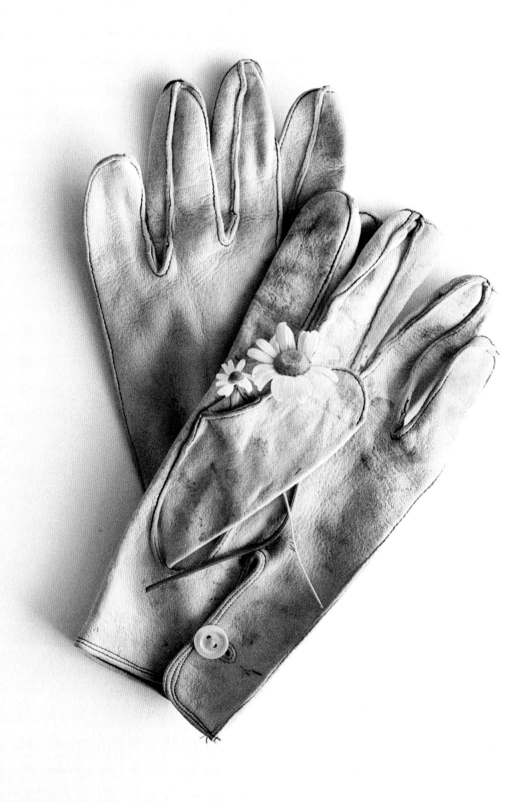

ON A FLOWER FARM It's easy to paint a perfect pastoral vision of country life, but as those who truly live it know, it's hard work that makes the country bloom. When I left my city floral studio, I went to work on my friend Siri's family flower farm. I lived in a cabin down a long dirt road, where I took showers outside under the pear tree and heated my water on the woodstove. I lost myself to the rhythm of farm life: harvesting flowers and wheeling barrows up and down the rows of zinnias, dahlias, sunflowers, and snapdragons. I joined Siri and her family for dinners of simple but outrageously good food, enjoyed on a little table nestled into the kitchen with a ceiling strung to the rafters with bunches of drying flowers to be sold during the winter.

My back ached, my nose freckled, and slowly, flowers started to sparkle for me again. The day of the farmers' market was my favorite of the week, and I relished the chance to lovingly display the bouquets I had helped pick and arrange. The city girl in me also loved the chance to put on a clean dress and see all the small-town sights. My bridal bouquets in New York started at 250 dollars, but at the farmers' market, we charged 12; the only difference was the lack of a silk ribbon and city real estate. To be honest, the country bouquets were better. I could wander the farm and find all sorts of unusual things to include, like a snare of wild blackberries, or some wispy grass whose movement added a breath of fresh air to otherwise upright stems. Of all the bouquets I've made, those are some of my favorites, and I love knowing that they ended up on kitchen tables, being admired over neighborly chatter and cups of morning coffee. A delightful fate for a country bouquet and a satisfying sojourn for a florist–turned–farm girl.

Opposite: My gardening gloves, which I rarely remember to wear. I just like to have my hands in the dirt.

HOW TO
ARRANGE FLOWERS
LIKE A FARM GIRL

I.

Pick the flowers yourself, even if it means
forgoing big, showy blooms.

2.

Look for interesting foliage that's
nuanced in color, beyond only green.

3.

Use flowering herbs, vegetables,
and all sorts of textural elements.

4.

Include unopened buds, full blooms,
and seedpods all from the same flower
for botanical interest.

5.

Don't fuss. Farm girls swish everything
together loosely without too much worry.

6.

Plop a tied bouquet in a mason jar or
old pitcher on the kitchen table.

7.

Invite a friend over for a slice of pie,
and send them home with the flowers.
It's the neighborly thing to do.

Opposite: A silvery mix from the farm, including artichokes and artichoke foliage, dusty miller,
black scabiosa, dried poppy pods, carrot flowers, yarrow, purple sage, grapes on the vine, and a host
of other small textural bits that make this bouquet wholly wild.

Elmwood, our meadow, and my beloved sister.

ELMWOOD

Elmwood is my family's summerhouse, ours since 1807. This means that the attics (three) are filled with a mix of forgotten badminton sets, butterfly nets, boxes of nineteenth-century family journals, broken chairs, childhood toys, old mattresses, two hundred years' worth of family photos, countless puzzles missing just one piece, a very perplexing Victorian bathing suit, and a trunk full of botanical plant specimens pressed by my great-great-grandmother in 1873.

The house is situated on the edge of our own little peninsula, so water and meadow surround us on three sides, with views of New Hampshire's weatherworn granite mountains rumpled in the distance. I'm deeply attached to the meadow and its numerous wildflowers, whose growth I track each morning with steadfast determination not often applied elsewhere in my life. The little flowing brook, pond, and eventual river that wind alongside our fifty-seven acres are a source of daily solace in the canoe, and only from the water can we snatch a good view of the sunset through our pine woods. No neighbors can be seen in any direction, although we are just a short drive from our tiny, one-stop-sign town, where there is an old-fashioned market selling local goat cheese (the baying of goats is audible from the register) and a singularly delicious ginger ice cream, along with the canned vegetables, hot dog buns, and bug spray that seem to populate all country stores.

At home, there are two kitchens and two stoves—although, mysteriously, one kitchen has both and the other has none. One stove is a hulking cast-iron cookstove, and I wonder if the kitchen was erected around it, as it seems impossible that it would fit through any door. If we ever wanted to remove it, we'd likely have to burn the house down, and the way the stove smokes, it does feel like the fire department should immediately be summoned. (I've called them only once, though.) A chalkboard hangs in that same red gingham kitchen, detailing the family history in bullet-point form, starting with George Robinson's arrival from Scotland in 1642 and noting important dates like historic floods. The house may have ten different coffeemakers, but we are lucky if one works. There are several generations of toasters and a collection of prehistoric crumbs. The wallpaper is peeling in places; some windows are painted shut. Cracks and crevices abound; chipmunks sometimes play house alongside us. I panic at the thought of anyone "improving" anything.

Each of the seven bedrooms has a different spirit. There is my parents' room, the butterfly room, situated right off the front door. It's the most elegantly appointed, with a bay window and in clear earshot of all who enter and exit. Directly

above that is the lilac room, named both for its purple flowery wallpaper and the view outside its westward windows in May. It has an especially lovely white chenille bedspread, bleached by the sun. This is my sister's room, and it is also where we put guests, as it has the most comfortable mattress and a captivating view. It might also be where we secretly kissed our boyfriends as teenagers. Across the hall is the morning glory bedroom, the wiener dog children's room, and the potentially haunted stencil room. The hallway has filmy Swiss dot curtains that remind me of an Andrew Wyeth painting, curtain billowing in the breeze.

The smallest bedroom hangs off a long corridor at the far end of the ground floor so that it sits undisturbed next to the meadow outside. Its proportions are not unlike those of a closet, but it has the undisputed best view. This little room is mine. From my pillow (with its antique, lace-trimmed case), I can watch the moon rising over the lake and see a thousand stars glow over the mountains. Birds and wildflowers flirt outside. The bed itself is no wider than my pillow—an old metal cot, even smaller than a single; the very same bed where my great-great-grandmother slept. (I do hope she had a different mattress; you can feel each spring in this one.) The walls are sky-blue plaster, threaded with lace-like cracks; every summer, my mother advances with a spackled putty knife, and every summer, I hold her off. There is a small white writing desk and a white bedside table. The view outside the window is more beautiful to me than even the grandest of sights imaginable. (I'm not entirely sure why, but looking at a view through a window frame is somehow more intimate than seeing the very same view outside.)

I don't remember whose idea it was to keep my grandfather's ashes inside the grandfather clock, but it was a good one. Nor do I know how this house has existed well into the twenty-first century without a washing machine, effective heating, or more than one bathroom. What I do know is that our property is edged with a thousand wild blueberry bushes, and the forest is carpeted with native lady's slipper orchids. The surrounding water shines black, dotted with golden water lilies and purple blooming pickerelweed in summer, and bass swim alongside beavers and turtles. Over two hundred bird species migrate through our treetops. The sun rises across the meadow and the lake each day from behind our favorite mountain, and we wake up early to see it. The stars thickly sparkle in the darkest nights I have ever seen, and we make a point to stay up late to watch comets shoot past. It's a real country house, held together by sheer love, many layers of white paint, and a little breeze.

A single red geranium to match Elmwood's gingham kitchen is an offering on the altar of country.

Flowers freshly picked from the garden, left just as I picked them, in an old ketchup bottle,
a drinking glass, a mason jar, and a porcelain pitcher.

The kitchen table and assorted chairs were dragged outside, under the candle-strung apple tree, for my thirtieth birthday party.

A screen door slamming closed is one of my favorite country sounds.

Lady's slipper orchids
and moss.

An Oriental poppy, sprung
from the garden.

Cosmos to make a grown woman cry,
with a veil of wild clematis.

A sign of home.

Above: A favorite bottle from Elmwood.

Opposite: The meadow, distilled into bottles, under a portrait of the house. Along the mantel, from left to right, are goldenrod, wild grass, milkweed, echinacea, chamomile, Queen Anne's lace, yarrow, dog daisies, plum poppy, and black-eyed Susans.

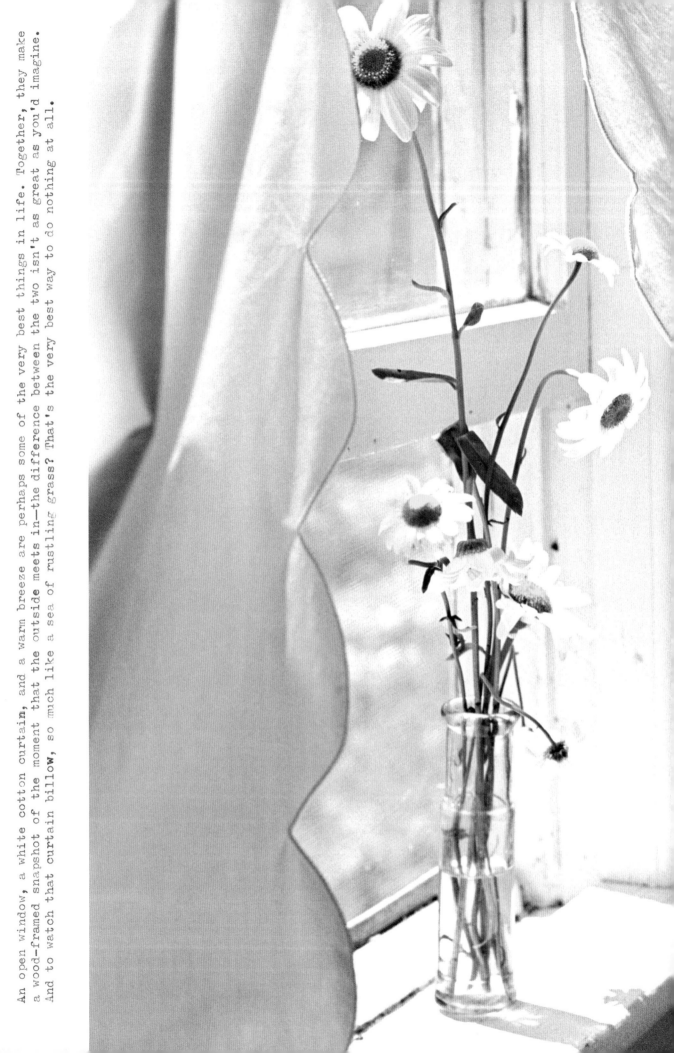

An open window, a white cotton curtain, and a warm breeze are perhaps some of the very best things in life. Together, they make a wood-framed snapshot of the moment that the outside meets in—the difference between the two isn't as great as you'd imagine. And to watch that curtain billow, so much like a sea of rustling grass? That's the very best way to do nothing at all.

COUNTRY THINGS TO DO

Pick your own flowers.

Dry your sheets in the sun.

Set a dinner table under the stars.

Enter a flower arrangement in the county fair.

Go barefoot.

Use a gingham tablecloth.

Collect scented geraniums.

Throw a party on the solstice.

Learn to identify birdcalls.

Grow edible flowers.

Support your local farmers.

Have an honor-system flower stand.

Collect leaves on walks.

Go to a barn dance.

Drive with the windows down.

Drink your morning coffee in a garden.

Learn a cake recipe by heart.

Feed the birds.

Keep a pair of clippers in your car.

Leave a nice surprise in your neighbor's mailbox.

Remember to look for shooting stars.

FANCY

THINGS

Fancy is a word that flirts on the edge of ridiculousness, but please indulge me when I use it. Little indulgent pleasures are precisely what fanciness is all about—the inessential glimmers that exist only for enjoyment. And what could better fit that bill than garden flowers, the ones we worship by pinching and pruning to coax them into our utmost ideals of perfection. The luscious varieties, the feminine roses and eye-popping peonies, the fragrant sorts that are best suited to being tied up with streaming silk ribbons, swathed in pale pink tissue, corseted in golden paper, and sent to profess undying love.

Fancy flowers can bloom in unexpected places: on the most delicate bone china, embroidered onto an evening gown, sparkling on the wrist of a hostess as she raises her champagne flute. Then, of course, there is the opulence of a well-set table, heaving with a bounty of blooms—often considered the highest calling for so many of our beloved fancy flowers. As a party florist, I've strewn tables with more flowers than I thought they could hold and hung a thousand votive candles from cherry

blossom canopies conjured into life in New York ballrooms. I've watched the taper candles drip low and cast a spell over centerpieces until the individual colors and shapes of the flowers themselves no longer mattered but the whole tablescape radiated a magic beyond what any single arrangement could dream of achieving in full sun.

I've always felt a pull toward beauty and the feeling of specialness just beyond what we experience in our everyday lives. As a little girl, I ached for petticoats and picnics with pink lemonade in cut-crystal glasses in Victorian greenhouses, iced petits fours on little china plates and flowers tucked into my hair. The link between flowers and beauty and pleasure was clear even then. And now, to wear floral silk whenever I like, or buy bunches of roses as often as possible, or simply bask in the glow of candlelight when a little magic is needed—these are simply the sweetest luxuries of my life. I do think true fanciness is a feeling more than anything specific, an ever-shifting desire and longing for beauty. And what could be more overwhelmingly beautiful than a bouquet of flowers?

AMERICAN C

To ANNUAL DUES FOR
To Sustaining Member

To Gift 1960 V
To Gift M

Please mail your remittance, payable to
AMERICAN CAMELLIA SOCIETY, in this envelope

Members in Foreign Countries may pay their dues through one of our
representatives:

G. H. Pinckney, % John Waterer Sons & Crisp, Ltd.,
    Twyford, Berks, England. (£ 2. 3. 0.)

Hazlewood Bros., Pty. Ltd.
    Box 1, Epping, N. S. W., Australia.

Felix M. Jury,
    Takorangi, Waitara, Taranaki, New Zealand.

AMY MERRICK

N°5
CHANEL
PARIS

Flowers

Hermès silk flowers might be the most expensive bouquet I'll ever buy, but sometimes lifelong botanical bliss is worth the splurge.

FANCY

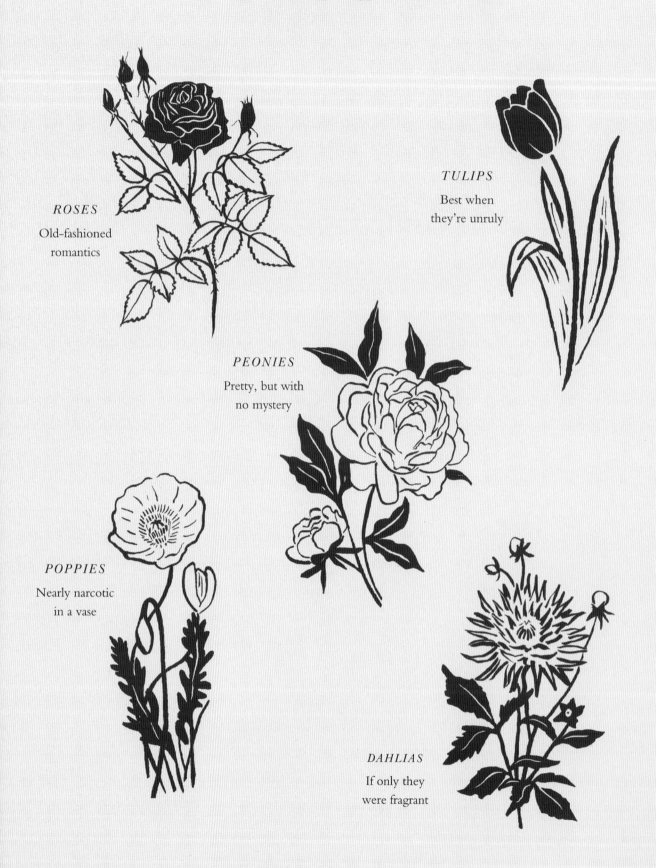

ROSES
Old-fashioned
romantics

TULIPS
Best when
they're unruly

PEONIES
Pretty, but with
no mystery

POPPIES
Nearly narcotic
in a vase

DAHLIAS
If only they
were fragrant

What makes a flower fancy?

FLOWERS

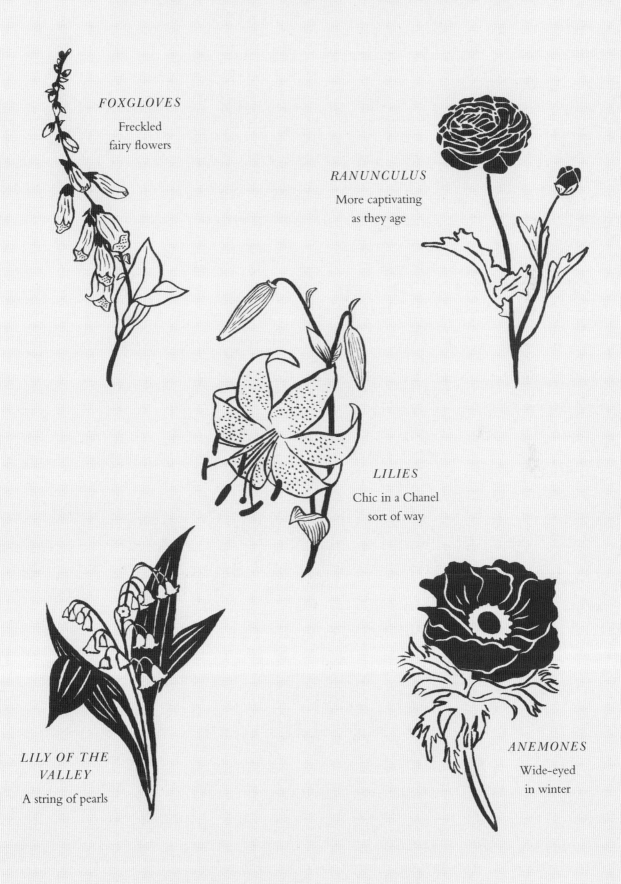

FOXGLOVES

Freckled
fairy flowers

RANUNCULUS

More captivating
as they age

LILIES

Chic in a Chanel
sort of way

**LILY OF THE
VALLEY**

A string of pearls

ANEMONES

Wide-eyed
in winter

If a stem seduces you so entirely that you cannot help but take her home.

A FLOWER AND HER PERFUME

Is there anything more heavenly than to smell like a flower? The scent dabbed onto the soft skin of your neck, just behind your earlobe—a place only those closest can smell. The classic perfume Joy requires ten thousand jasmine buds and twenty-eight dozen roses to fill a small bottle. Imagine all those blooms distilled into an old-fashioned crystal glass placed on a mirrored vanity. Thousands of flowers with only a single spritz.

Fragrance is an allure more dearly bought than even the most luxurious French perfume, though, as fragrant flowers are often the most ephemeral. It is a worthy sacrifice, scent in lieu of long life; it's their redolence that captivates us entirely, entangling nostalgia and romance in a single heady cocktail. Even just a few stems on a bedside table can entirely perfume your dreams.

Opposite: Magnolia grandiflora sparkling in the sun.

Day one: tulips looking very sweet.

Day nine: tulips looking rather sexy.

A VASE OF CONSEQUENCE, AND A SINGLE BREATHTAKING DAHLIA.

The two could nearly drown you in beauty. This Frances Palmer vase is like a pair of indulgent shoes: whatever you put in it becomes chic. How do you know if you have a vase of consequence? If the thought of breaking it breaks your heart.

Vases by the incomparable potter Frances Palmer, whose friendship has encouraged me since my earliest days as a florist.

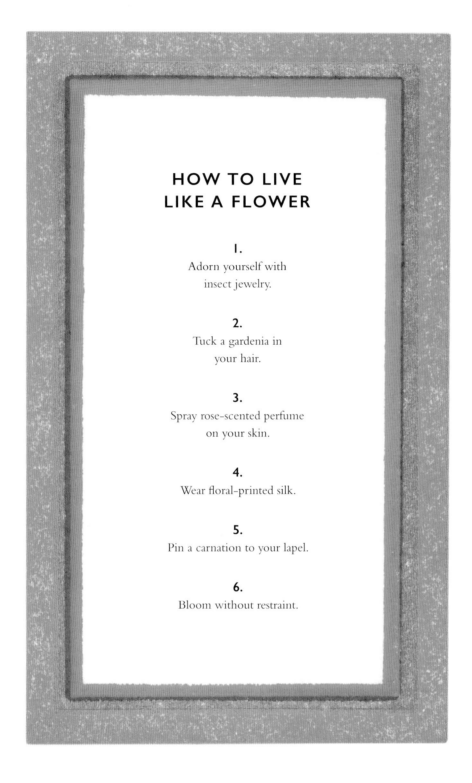

HOW TO LIVE
LIKE A FLOWER

1.
Adorn yourself with
insect jewelry.

2.
Tuck a gardenia in
your hair.

3.
Spray rose-scented perfume
on your skin.

4.
Wear floral-printed silk.

5.
Pin a carnation to your lapel.

6.
Bloom without restraint.

Opposite: I'm not afraid of spiders when they're 1940s amethyst.

Ogawa Kazumasa's hand-colored photo of cherry blossoms, 1897.

Peonies have one flaw:
they're perfect.

Other than that,
they're perfect.

'Quick, someone! The *big* vases!'

An illustration by Lesley Blanch
from "Hostess" by Constance Spry.

A little cutie.

Peonies, sweet pea, and some ravishing, nearly watercolored tulips, arranged with a flower frog.

Dear Lily of the Valley,

Wherever I see you and whenever I smell you, you take me immediately to the dappled shade underneath my favorite maple trees at home. Along woodland edges, your little white pearls are strung on an endless green silk thread. You are happy there and it shows: you've run rampant through all the places with the very best views. Your smell is more transporting than a first-class plane ticket, more nostalgic than even a whiff of my mother's perfume. Your essence cannot be distilled, though perfumers have been trying for a thousand years. I admire that about you.

You are the answer to the question everyone asks, the little secret I like to keep. My favorite flower?

You.

THE RICHNESS OF ROSES

Put out of your mind those long-stemmed, graceless, unscented pretenders: they are just shadows of what a rose can be. A real rose ravishes, blowsy and intoxicating with velvety petals cupped or gently folded. Its fragrance can distill the essence of spun sugar, warm honey, or ripe fruit, spicy sweet tea or a heady musk. The very best roses defy description; they smell of nothing more or less than deeply, luxuriantly of themselves.

Roses are unmatched, the absolute queens of flowers. They are ruffled explosions of everything that is bewitchingly feminine in this world, but when you go closer, they aren't the helpless beauties you'd imagine. Their enchantment also ensnares, as they are the only flowers capable of drawing blood. Thorns are a plea for privacy, and a prick from a rose is a swollen souvenir that often lasts longer than the life of a flower itself. Human hands have known that throb since the first roses were nudged into cultivation over five thousand years ago.

Roses oiled the bodies of Egyptians, decorated the crowns of the Greeks, and were promiscuously strewn over the dining tables and beds of the Romans. They perfumed the air of the paradise gardens in the Middle East, and they, too, were conquered by the Crusaders. Roses were tended by monks in medicinal herb gardens, then adorned altars in honor of the Virgin Mary. They were both revered as transcendent and reviled as extravagant. They've been painted and woven and forged and carved and cast into ubiquity. No matter where you are, a rose is a rose is a rose. They are perhaps the single flower whose name is known by all.

Roses thrive best in a garden of their own, without competition from other plants. They like space to bloom, to spread, to climb or ramble, and their thorns exist to keep small animals that are attracted to their scented blooms from ripping them to bits. In the garden, they can be moody and temperamental, with demanding needs and well-defined dislikes. They require

pruning and cajoling to put on a spectacular show, and compliments don't hurt either. When they are nurtured and satisfied, they reward their admirers like no other flower. They make you work for their affection; they have mastered the art of allure.

As cut flowers, though, they can be similarly high maintenance. They don't flourish in vases; like unhappy canaries in gilt cages, they simply refuse to sing for long. Some heirloom varieties last only a day. But what a day it is! Their ephemerality is actually their most generous gift; they contain the full potency of an entire lifetime distilled into a single deep, delicious breath. Should you require further persuasion to join in the cultish adoration, a quick glance at any nearby rose catalog will make your pulse race. The naming of roses is a love affair unto itself: the French roses—Perle d'Or, Pompon de Paris, Gloire de Dijon—conjure supreme elegance. Dozens of varieties are named after extravagantly sumptuous countesses or duchesses or madames; those hold court among the most ruffled, fragrant specimens. Then there are the English roses whose names praise virtue: the Lark Ascending, Dainty Bess, the Shepherdess, the Poet's Wife. The more modern roses say it all, and a bit more explicitly: Passionate Kisses, Eyes for You, Deep Secret, and Hanky Panky don't even try to obscure their enticement. Not that roses need to hide their charms—they bloom only to seduce.

Bees can often be seen flying drunkenly away from roses, colliding in midair, giddy and lovestruck after a fling. And isn't it nice to know that what smells divine to us also smells divine to a bee? That potent scent, so intoxicating to a human nose, must utterly overwhelm a bee's impossibly small being. A rose's voluptuous, tousled petals and pollen-dusted lashes must be a bee paradise, like swimming in a pool of silk velvet. Oh to be a bee, completely enveloped in a rose. That must be the most luxurious feeling of all.

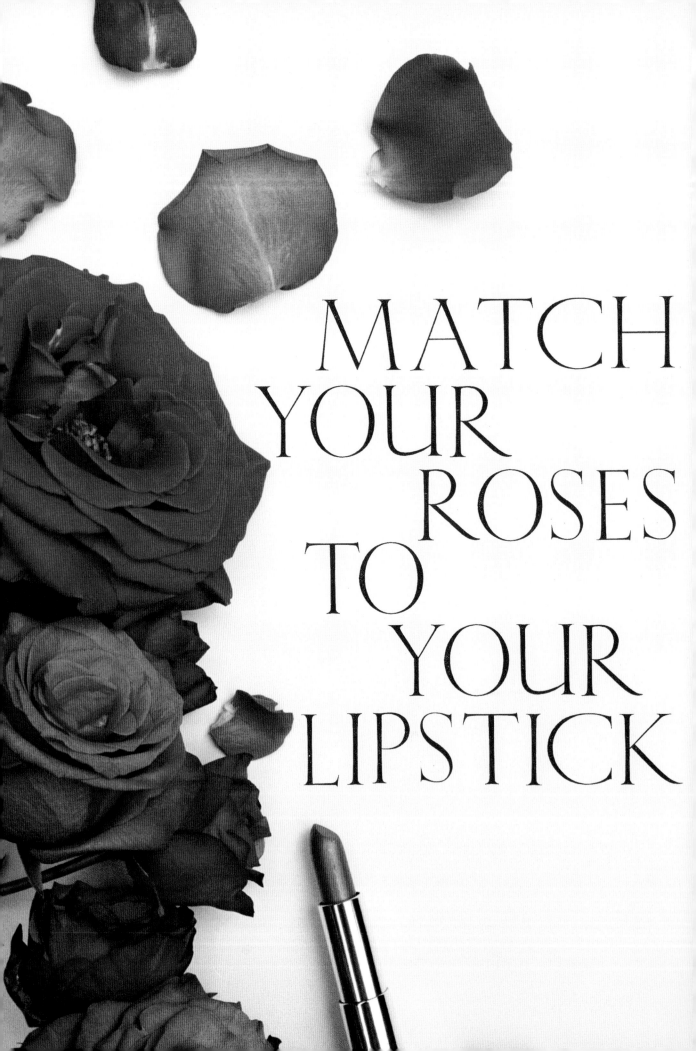

MATCH YOUR ROSES TO YOUR LIPSTICK

HOW TO
TURN A BATHTUB
INTO A VASE

I.

Take a shower beforehand; it's worth it to rise out of
the bath relaxed, without worrying about washing.

2.

Draw a just-too-hot bath.

3.

Drip fragrant oil into the water, and light candles.

4.

Float handfuls of loose petals, and scatter
a few whole flowers.

5.

Open a delicious book, preferably a paperback.

6.

Soak in your most exquisite outfit, the one you were
born to wear. (You are the flower in this vase.)

Opposite: A camellia taking her bath.

Above: Pleated silk and golden fringe.

Opposite: Icelandic poppies on black velvet.

CARNATION APPRECIATION

Carnations are the darlings of many a cheap flower stand. People assume they're ordinary, but if you had never seen one before, how beautiful would you find a single stem? A profusion of petals so heavily ruffled you might imagine they inspired a 1920s Russian ballet skirt, a stem so like a dancer's limbs: long, strong, but impossibly lithe. Maybe you'd lift the fresh carnation to your nose and smell its true scent—a heavy, rich, spiced clove, so unlike the fragrance of any other flower. You'd admire each petal, painstakingly edged with the most delicate hand-cut fringe, each leaf the

perfectly coupled curl of a birthday-present bow. You might think carnations were beautiful, if only they weren't everywhere.

I hadn't thought too much about carnations until the day I got a message that Oscar de la Renta had died. I had always deeply admired Mr. de la Renta's work, his absolute elegance, generosity of spirit, and total celebration of strong, sophisticated femininity. He was a man who clearly loved and respected women, and you could see it in his clothes. He was also, as it turns out, a man who loved flowers. Just a few months before I got the news of his

passing, I had been hired by a client to send Mr. de la Renta a thank-you bouquet. I made it quite wild, as I figured he was usually sent fussy, overly luxurious arrangements. My tactic worked; I heard the next day that he adored the flowers and took them directly home to his wife—the highest compliment he could give, as she was known for her exceptional taste. Could I possibly put together some arrangements for a private dinner that weekend?

I could, and did, and I will never forget the name cards that graced that table of twelve. Oh to be a peony in that bouquet, to attend the many parties my flowers have been invited to! I never met Mr. de la Renta, but he met me—he saw right into my heart through the bouquets I arranged.

When he passed away, I created arrangements with dark crimson carnations for the family's private gathering. Carnations were his favorite, they said. Learning this touched me deeply—a flower so humble, so common, and yet he could see through the plastic wrapping to know a carnation's truth: utter glamour, hiding in plain sight. I often buy myself a bunch and think of him.

I spent a white-gloved afternoon in the archive of the British Museum, marveling at eighteenth-century floral collages by Mary Delaney.

The lavishness of abundance.

The elegance of restraint.

For the price of a bottle of wine, you could easily buy a bunch of flowers. Either would flush your cheeks, ease your tightly wound worries, and give unrestrained pleasure. All you'd have to do is drink them in. One would intoxicate for an evening, the other for an entire week—sipped slowly until the last petal drops. It's quite possible to be drunk on flowers; I feel tipsy all the time.

FANCY THINGS TO DO

Count rose petals.

Dress up to visit gardens.

Buy more flowers than you can carry.

Write thank-you notes on personalized stationery.

Slip sachets into dresser drawers.

Write love letters.

Spritz those letters with floral perfume.

Go to the ballet.

Keep fragrant flowers by your bedside.

Toast with real crystal champagne coupes.

Tie bouquets with silk ribbon.

Eat from floral china dessert plates.

Watch tulips twist.

Buy a first edition of a beloved book.

Host a proper dinner party.

Sleep on ironed pillowcases.

Collect beautiful vases.

Treat yourself to afternoon tea.

Decorate a cake with icing roses.

Bury your face in peonies.

Gild the lily.

HUMBLE

PLEASURES

I worry that humble flowers don't always get the admiration they should, but then again, humble flowers ask for no admiration at all. They simply bloom as they are, whether they're tended or not. The first crocus of the year is a humble flower, its soft yellow petals pushing out of the muddy ground, delicate and shivering. But don't be fooled into thinking that the little yellow crocus is lowly; it takes amazing strength to withstand winter's last frigid gasps.

It's strange and wonderful that after so many years as a fancy florist, I now find the most joy in a handful of wild, tousled daisies picked under the sun. I'm drawn to the simple ones, the wild and free beauties who effortlessly weave throughout meadows, gather in drifts at woodland edges, and run rampant along so many roadsides. A bunch of fragrant violets is a just a trifle, but also a priceless one—their sweetness can't be bought in any store. (And it is a true labor of love to pick even a small bunch.) Similarly, dandelion seed pods are rarer to find in an arrangement than the most frilly, flagrant peonies, because one false move and they're fluff in the wind. Of all the humble treasures, though, I suspect four-leaf clovers are the holy grail. People often fret that they never seem to find them, but the trick is simply persistence.

I feel similarly about luck: fortune favors those who bend down to look for it.

We all start off humble, completely unafraid to admit how much we don't know. Where do clouds come from? Why do leaves change color in the autumn? Why do flowers die? It's only as we grow older that we stop asking the questions that make us feel small. The more I observed the whole of the natural world, not just overtly beautiful flowers, the greater the sense of amazement I felt toward all things both humble and grand.

The word *humble* is derived from the Latin *humus*, which means "the ground." It's only fitting, then, that flowers spring forth from the soil, rooted in humility from the very start. To be humble is not to be timid or passive but to ground yourself in the knowledge of how much you have yet to grow.

BUTTERCUPS
AND DAISIES

14

Weasel Snout or Yellow Deadnettle (Galeobdolon luteum) scale 2/5

15

Hairy Brome (Bromus asper)   scale 2/5

The first crocus of spring, kissed with melting snow.

HUMBLE

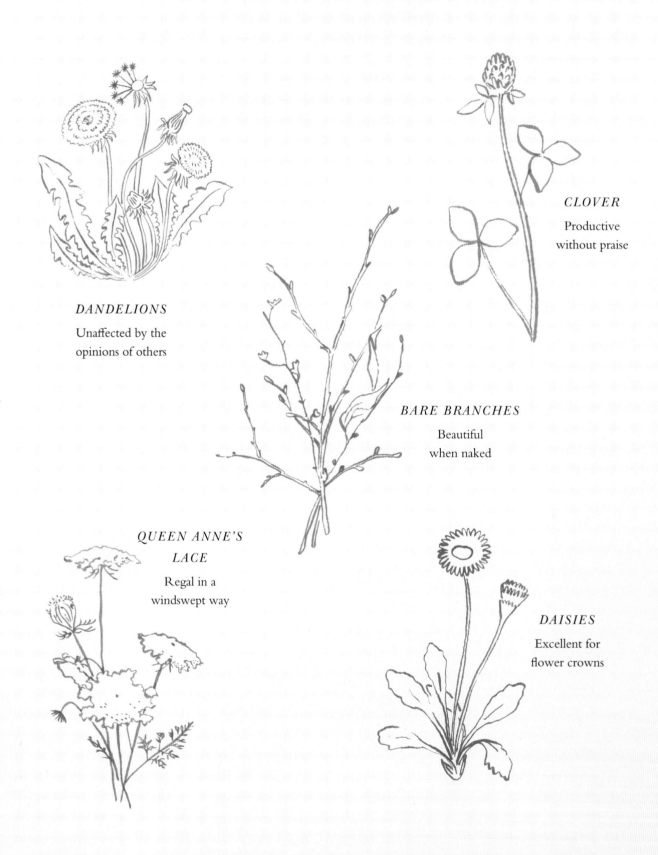

DANDELIONS
Unaffected by the opinions of others

CLOVER
Productive without praise

BARE BRANCHES
Beautiful when naked

QUEEN ANNE'S LACE
Regal in a windswept way

DAISIES
Excellent for flower crowns

There is a fine line between a wildflower and a weed.

FLOWERS

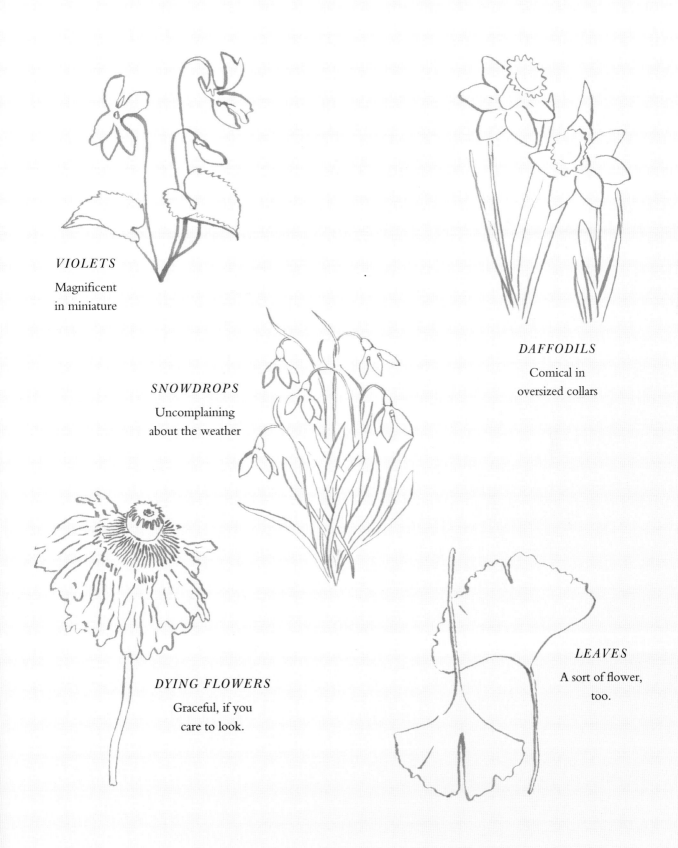

VIOLETS

Magnificent
in miniature

DAFFODILS

Comical in
oversized collars

SNOWDROPS

Uncomplaining
about the weather

DYING FLOWERS

Graceful, if you
care to look.

LEAVES

A sort of flower,
too.

It's a line I like to cross often.

WHAT IS A FLOWER? We find ourselves on page 164 of this book but haven't yet thought about what flowers even are. Or why we're innately attracted to them, or why they exist at all. Flowers are simply a biological necessity, like the sensation of human love.

Flowers exist solely as a means for reproduction, a delicate natural romance meant only for the birds and bees. Our admiration is just collateral damage; we're caught in the crossfire of pollination, interlopers of the highest order. It's wonderful to realize that the rules of attraction hold true for all living creatures, that butterflies and humans both are drawn to flirt with the very same blooms. Flowers are cunning in their enticement—scent, color, pattern, and nectar are all their instruments of attraction. The speckles on the throat of a foxglove are a landing strip illuminated for bees, a "Follow the dots, please" to show them where to enter. The yellow center of a daisy is a "Land here, please" bull's-eye seen at a distance.

When we talk about flowers, we talk about sex and love, life and death, and rebirth, too. It is humbling to remember that they do not bloom for us.

Opposite: A magnolia spilling her heart out.

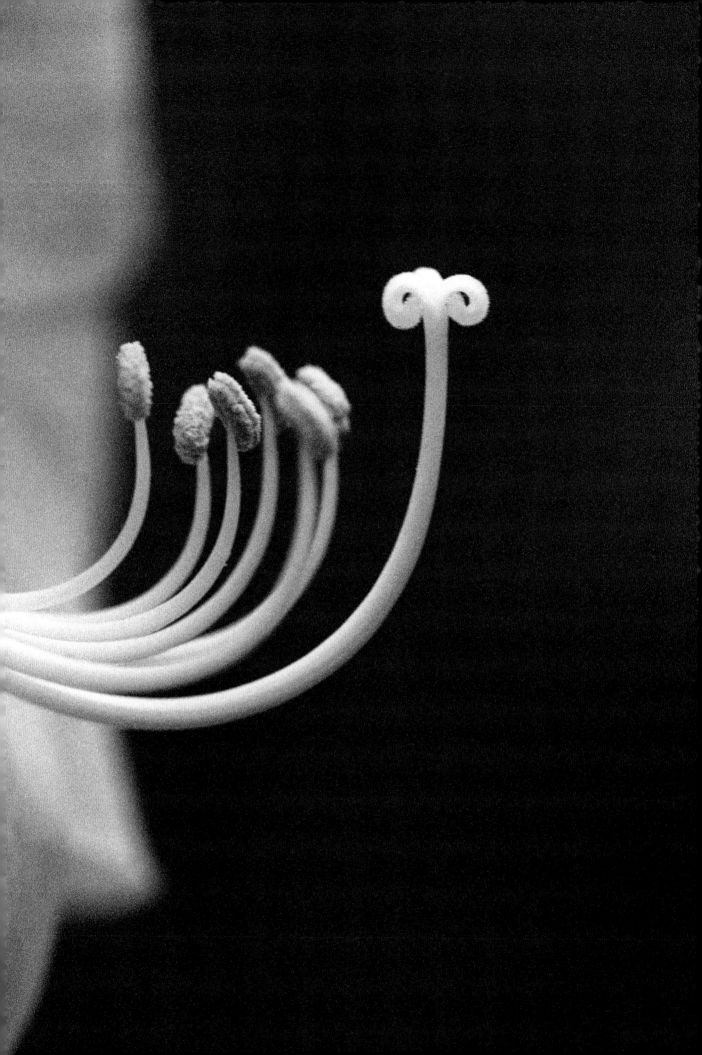

THE PARTS OF
A FLOWER

THE PISTIL

The female anatomy: the central
column consisting of the stigma, style, and ovary.
The stigma sits at the very tip of the style,
which connects to the flower at the ovary,
where ovules develop into seeds after fertilization.

THE STAMEN

The male anatomy: pollen-covered
anthers held in place by long filaments.
Pollen is transferred to the stigma for fertilization
by pollinators such as bees, insects, or birds,
or even by the wind.

SEPALS

The leaflike green encasements that
protect a flower while it is in bud and open to
form the base structure of the flower.
As a unit, the sepals are called the calyx.

PETALS

The means of protection for the sex
organs of a flower. Petals can be brightly colored,
patterned, or scented to attract pollinators.
A group of petals collectively is called the corolla.

Opposite: The most intimate parts of an amaryllis, on display for all to see.

Above: This arrangement arranged itself. I picked some yellowing ferns and grasses, a stem of fennel, some black-eyed Susans, and some vines whose name I don't know. They looked so beautiful unarranged that I put them in my vase just as they were. I don't think I could arrange something as spontaneous as this even if I tried.

Opposite: A blade of grass drawn by Fritz Kühn, from his 1952 book *In My Grassfolder,* which I return to often for inspiration.

THE WISH-MAKERS

I never imagined that you could buy a humble thing like a dandelion, but you can and I have. It was a rare variety, bought in an exquisite shop selling only the most unusual wildflowers. It was a splurge but beautiful; its saw-toothed leaves were intricately cut, much deeper and with sharper blades than those on the yard flowers of my youth; those dandelions always seemed to possess a very average mustard-on-lettuce color scheme, with a puff whose only purpose was to supply wishes for an eight-year-old. But both are rare or commonplace, depending on whether your yard is in Hokkaidō or rural New Hampshire.

Dandelions are often derided by that graceless word *weed* and unceremoniously yanked at every turn. They're free-spirited and independent; they don't need to be pollinated in order to float their seeds into the sky. This accounts for much of their success in maddening lawn purists, but it wasn't always so, as they were purposefully introduced to North America for their medicinal benefits. The entire plant, from root to flower, is edible: dandelion wine, roasted root tea, salad leaves, and steeped flowers—all are ways you can imbibe some yellow sunshine. And yellow is not a prerequisite either. There are

creamy white dandelions, bright pink ones, and my favorite: a pale pink with a soft buttery yellow center, called *Taraxacum pseudoroseum*. I shudder to think that anyone could be so cruel as to pull its pinky rose rays, so like the colors of the earliest sunrise, from the ground.

When seen with gentler eyes, dandelions become impossibly charming, with their distinctive leaves and a shaggy golden lion's mane that opens and closes with the sun, earning them the nickname fairy clocks. When it's time for seed dispersal, the flower magics itself into a cloud of downy deliciousness incapable of being captured for long. Dandelion seed puffs are some of the most delicate natural beauties, but I always love the most fragile things, like spiderwebs heavy with dew and dried leaves nibbled with lacelike holes.

While it may seem impossible to transport, a dandelion puff, if picked while it's still in bud, will open in water—the most ephemeral flower a vase can hold. The legend of wish fulfillment is perhaps a dandelion's simplest sweetness, though: a single blow and your thoughts and dreams are carried away on the wind by nothing more than a humble weed.

Everyday dandelions.

An expensive dandelion, but it doesn't know that.

My grandmother picked a small handful of violets growing on a grassy hillside outside her family's home on April 19, 1947. She pinned them to the breast of her simple white suit and married my grandfather in front of a judge, a civil ceremony with very little fuss. I'm not sure I can imagine a more romantic flower.

SWEET VIOLET.—*Viola odorata.*

TREE SKELETONS More people should appreciate the beauty of bare branches—their architectural allure creates an extraordinary backbone when everything else is bleak. Trees are like people; some are just more beautiful when naked. I often think that the wide spread of a bare canopy looks like the spread of roots in the soil, or perhaps flashes of lightning in the sky. Birds' nests are exposed; nuances in bark become significant. In midwinter, bare branches are like line drawings in a vase, and if the water is kept fresh, little leaves will often sprout indoors. Don't think for a moment that just because branches are bare, they aren't alive.

Opposite: One branch of wild plum in winter, waiting to burgeon indoors.

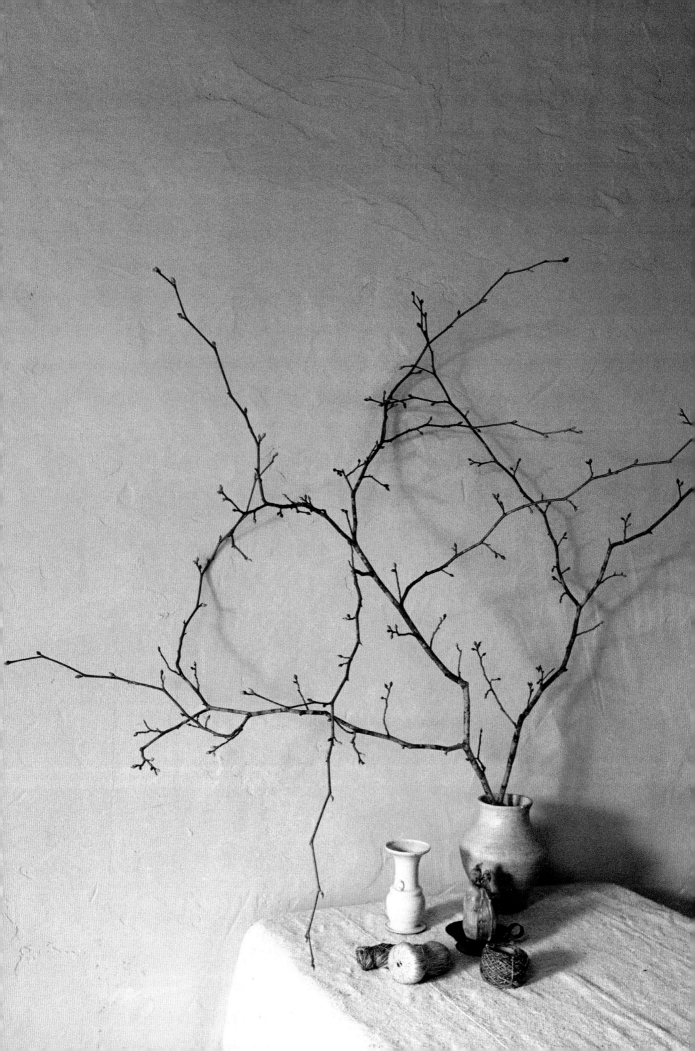

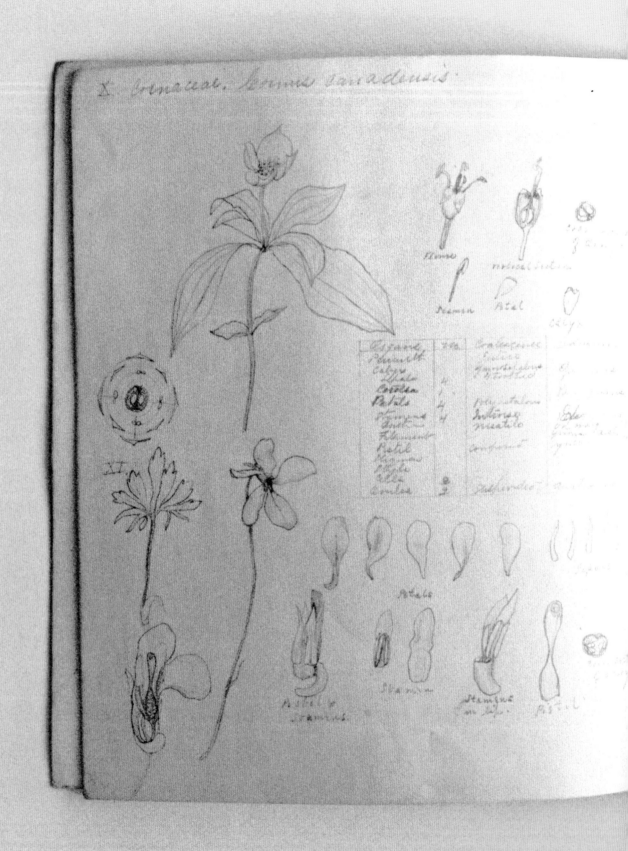

My great-great-grandmother Ella Averill Robinson was a botany student at Wellesley College in 1876.
These are drawings from her botanical sketchbooks, each illustrating a New England wildflower.

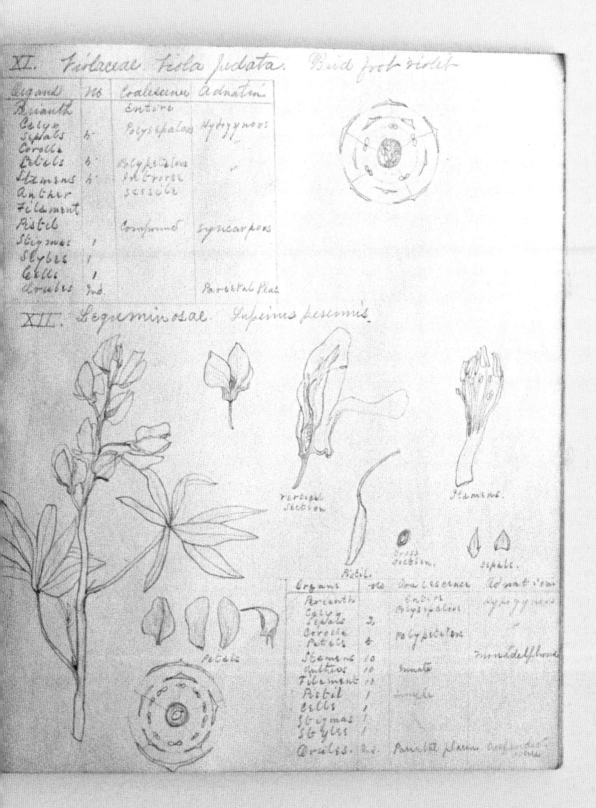

XI. Violaceae. Viola pedata. Bird foot violet

Organs	No	Coalescence	Adnation
Perianth		Entire	
Calyx			
Sepals	5	Polysepalous	Hypogynous
Corolla			"
Petals	5	Polypetalous	
Stamens	5	Introrse	"
Anther		sessile	
Filament			
Pistil		Compound	Syncarpous
Stigmas	1		
Styles	1		
Cells	1		
Ovules	ind.		Parietal Plac

XII. Leguminosae. Lupinus perennis.

Vertical Section

Stamens.

Cross Section.

sepals.

Pistil.

Petals

Organs	No	Coalescence	Adnation
Perianth		Entire	Hypogynous
Calyx		Polysepalous	
Sepals	5		"
Corolla		Polypetalous	
Petals	5		
Stamens	10		Monadelphous
Anthers	10	innate	
Filament	10		
Pistil	1	simple	
Cells	1		
Stigmas	1		
Styles	1		
Ovules	ind.	Parietal placen	suspended ovules

HOW TO MAKE FLOWERS LAST FOREVER

1.
Keep a nature sketchbook.

2.
Press leaves and petals between the covers
of books. Weigh them down until dried.

3.
Paint the shadows cast by
flowers on paper.

4.
Make a sunprint with photoreactive
paper on a sunny day to see just how
abstract the shapes of leaves can be.

5.
Study a single flower so intently
that you never forget it.

Opposite: This is not a pressed daffodil but a paper collage from the eighteenth
century belonging to my friend Tania. Three hundred years old and fresh as a daisy.

DAFFODILS HAVE IMPECCABLE TIMING.

They bloom just when you cannot stand one more day of winter. To combine daffodils with other flowers, cut their stems and allow them to ooze their sap in a separate vase for an hour before using them in an arrangement. Here, all the sunny faces of spring sing in a small pot with a flower frog; wintersweet branches form a fragrant frame to showcase creamy narcissus, daffodils, and snowflake bulbs. The arching piece of dying grass is really the best thing here, though.

HOW
MANY
FOUR-LEAF
CLOVERS
CAN

YOU
SEE?

ARRANGING SHADOWS I have a tender-ness for shadows; for cool, veiled corners and pools of dappled shade. (I'm like some flowers in that regard; I wilt in hot sun.) Shadows are also like flowers—brief, ever-shifting little enchantments, always swaying and suddenly gone. I've taken to arranging shadows in the way that other people place bou-quets, watching them flicker with as much enjoyment as I take in the flowers themselves. Large shadows cast from little stems, or a tangle of shadows from an otherwise simple bunch. The romance between light and shadow is a delicate dance, and when they meet a flower, good luck not falling in love.

Opposite: The shadows of dandelions, daisies, and forsythia in the afternoon sun.

He loves me?

The only flower capable of predicting love.

Dandelions and daisies: soul mates in the dictionary and the dirt.

DANDELION

F. *dalmatique.* — L. *dalmatica* fem. of *Dalmaticus,* belonging to

), a mound, bank against water. *damm,* only in the derived *man,* to dam up; O. Fries. Fries. *dām.* ✛ Du. *dam,* Dan. *dam,* Swed. *damm,* G. *damm,* a dam, dike. *ammjan,* to dam up. ther, applied to animals. e word as Dame.

L.) M. E. *damage.*— *dommage*); cf. Prov. o Late L. **damnāti*-Late L. *damnāticus,* es.—L. *damnātus,* mn.

aria.) M. E. *da*-—Ital. *damasco.* *Dammeseq,* Da-Der. *damask-*ith gold (F. *n,* adj.). me.—O. F. of *domi-*

M. E. L. *dam*-L. *damnum,* loss, . i. § 762.) Cf. M. E. *dampen,* to ; E. Fries. *damp,* vapour.✛Du. *amp,* vapour, steam; Dan. *damp,* G. *dampf,* vapour; Swed. *damb,* dust. From the 2nd grade of Teut. **dempan—*, pt. t. **damp,* pp. **dumpano—,* as in M. H. G. *dimpfen, timpfen,* str. vb., to reek; cf. Swed. dial. *dimba,* str. vb., to reek. See Dumps.

Damsel. (F.—L.) M. E. *damosel.*— O. F. *dameisele,* a girl, fem. of *dameisel,* a young man, squire, page.—Late L. *domi-cellus,* a page, short for **dominicellus,* double dimin. of *dominus,* a lord. (Pages were often of high birth.)

Dance. (F.—O.H.G.) M. E. *daun-cen.*—O. F. *danser.*—O. H. G. *dansōn,* to drag along (as in a round dance).— O.H.G. *dans,* 2nd grade of *dinsen,* to pull, draw; allied to E. Thin. Cf. Goth. *at-thinsan,* to draw towards one.

Dandelion, a flower. (F.—L.) F. *dent de lion,* tooth of a lion; named from the jagged leaves.—L. *dent-em,* acc. of *dens,* tooth; *dē,* prep.; *leōnem,* acc. of *leo,* lion.

on ... as Pro ... also ... or of ... state, ... *deis, deys.*— A. F. ... a high table (Supp. to Gode ... *discum,* acc. of *discus,* a quoit, ... in Late L. a table.—Gk. δίσκος, a quoit, disc. See Disc.

Daisy. (E.) M. E. *dayēsyẹ* (4 sylla-bles). A. S. *dæges ēage,* eye of day, i. e. the sun, which it resembles.

Dale, a valley. (E.) M. E. *dale.*— A.S. *dæl* (pl. *dal-u*).✛ Icel. *dalr,* Dan. Swed. *dal,* a dale; Du. *dal;* Goth. *dal;* G. *thal;* also O. Slav. *dolŭ* (Russ. *dol'*); cf. Gk. θόλος, a vault. **Der.** *dell.*

Dally, to trifle. (F.—Teut.) M. E. *dalien,* to play, trifle.—A.F. *and* O.F. *dalier,* to converse, chat, pass the time in light converse (Bozon). Of Teut. origin; cf. Bavarian *dalen,* to speak and act as children (Schmeller); mod. G. (vulgar) *dahlen,* to trifle.

Dalmatic, a vestment. (F.—Dal-

127

THE LENGTH OF A DAY

My sister once suggested we do a silent meditation together, three days of contemplative
camping in the woods. She is an enchanting
earth-mother sort and no stranger to expe-
riences like these, while I am decidedly less
meditative, in the traditional sense at least. My
mind feels unemptyable, with too many ideas
and plans, worries and joys for me to quiet it
entirely, and though I've always prized alone
time for regeneration, I had never faced it
entirely empty-handed. We would bring no
books or journals, and no cameras or phones,
nothing to distract us from our own silence.

We packed our bags and set off by water,
paddling the family canoe to a small cove on the
distant edge of a large pond on our property,
setting up camp nestled on the pine-needle car-
pet of woods we both knew well. A large stone
fire circle would be the center of our meditation
experience (or experiment, depending on which
sister you asked). She knew how she would fill
her three days—with a mix of yoga and meditation. I didn't know exactly how I'd fill mine.

The first morning dawned sunny, a classic
New England summer day, mild and blue—

until the mosquitoes descended at dusk. I wan-
dered the woods and found a warm rock on
the lake's edge. Should I try to sit cross-legged
and clear my mind? The water was flooded
with blooming lavender pickerelweed, a native
aquatic wildflower whose spires rise into a purple haze floating on the surface. I lay down and
saw both bumblebees and honeybees, intently
moving from flower to flower. Upon closer
inspection, I saw that each bloom was made
up of a hundred tiny flowers with a hundred thread-like, pollen-dusted stamens. The
bees visited only the newly opened florets.
I watched as the tiny purple petals curled in
on themselves after a bee had visited, clos-
ing themselves for business. The bumblebees
feasted with astonishing efficiency when com-
pared to the honeybees, whose meandering
style made me rethink all I knew about the
work ethics of insects. I watched them without
thought of anything else, becoming a bit of a
bee myself. I couldn't mark the passing hours
other than by watching the sun move through
the sky, and I noticed how the purple flowers
were reflected in the black water's mirrored

surface: every flower had a shadowy twin shining back. There were twice as many flowers to see than I first thought.

I spent the rest of the day looking around me, and instead of emptying my mind, I filled it to the brim with all manner of little things I would never have seen otherwise. Verdant moss creeping slowly over granite rocks, lichen in shocking shades of yellow, chartreuse, silver, crimson, orange. Lying on the pine needles, I looked toward the craggy bark of our native pines and saw the strongest trunks swaying imperceptibly in the breeze. The more I looked, the more I could see. The next day passed in similar slow motion, and I lay down to look even closer; an inchworm, no larger than mechanical pencil lead, tiptoed past on a leaf the size of my thumbnail. I didn't even know that I could see something so small. I lay in the sun, eyes closed, feeling its radiating warmth on the back of my eyelids. I could sense the movements of the clouds as they passed over the sun. It was the first time I had ever made the distinct observation of how a cloud viscerally feels on my skin.

I caught sight of a pair of monarch butterflies dancing together, flitting so high that they passed the treetops; I was awestruck seeing their delicate wings carry them higher than I had imagined they could go. I went to watch the sunset on the edge of the wetland, and as I sat, a small coyote approached the blueberry bushes, just a dozen yards from me. He started yapping happily, eating the berries right off the branches. It's amazing who will accept you as an equal when you sit still, alone, for long enough outside. I went down to the water to rinse my face, and as I leaned over, I saw a little smudge there that wouldn't come off no matter how much I scrubbed. I felt the spot and realized that it was no smudge but instead an imperceptible indentation on the bridge of my nose casting a slight shadow. I had never noticed its presence in over thirty years of looking in a mirror, but I had seen it immediately in the mysterious moving reflection of the water. My eyes had become sharpened to see the smallest of details, and by looking at the world around me, I could see myself anew. After three days of silence, a single moment could stretch to contain an eternity.

Sometimes I wonder how many more summers I'll get to see. It's a bittersweet equation when I do some honest estimates. I could have forty more summers. But it could also be four, or seventy-four. Forty glimpses of the summer's first daisies, or forty chances to breathe in the first rose of the year. Forty afternoons under the canopy of our apple tree, the goldenrod meadow waving in the breeze. I imagine what it would be like if I knew only forty more times. How much, then, would I cherish each kiss? Forty suddenly seems like the smallest number I know. But how lucky are we, really, to live it all even once?

HUMBLE THINGS TO DO

Make a daisy crown.

Wake early to see a sunrise.

Wish on a dandelion.

Say thank you.

Wear white cotton.

Press flowers.

Smile at a stranger.

Notice birds' nests in bare branches.

Close your eyes and look at the sun.

Collect leaves.

Eat bread and butter.

Be quiet.

Send a letter.

Take a nap under a tree.

Find four-leaf clovers.

Write with a freshly sharpened pencil.

Wear an old sweater.

Spend a quiet rainy day at home.

Call a friend.

Learn the phases of the moon.

Watch a candle burn low.

GOING

FAR AWAY

When you've seen both the city and the country, and loved both the fancy and the humble, there is nothing left to do but go far away.

I didn't know exactly how long I would be gone, or even where I would go, but I knew there was more to learn about flowers in places I had never been. I sensed that I still had a few more lives yet to live, and I didn't want to waste a moment on the old ones.

I bought a one-way plane ticket and packed a bag. (It's how all the best adventures start.) Luck was on my side; I had established a flexible business, so if I needed to teach a flower-arranging class or write a small article to fuel my travels, I could.

My curiosity led me to the cactus bloom in the Sonoran desert and to California's Death Valley to see wild poppies in profusion. I traveled to Morocco to wander tiled paradise gardens and to Spain to sun myself in stuccoed courtyards full of oranges, pomegranates, and geraniums in terra-cotta pots piled up to the roof. In France, I taught a floral workshop at a château where I strewed the halls with garden roses, and I took myself to Romania afterward to marvel at the folk-crafted flowers that were painted, carved, and embroidered onto every surface in the small villages of Maramureş. In Egypt, I stood in awe of ancient pink-painted frescoes of papyrus and lotus, and in Thailand, I bought garlands of jasmine and orchids to drape over my mosquito-netted four-poster bed. In Scotland, I swooned over endless rolling hills of heather, dotted with foxgloves, and in England, I completely lost my heart to a country with a passion for gardens and flowers unlike anywhere else in the world. I apprenticed at a wild, eccentric garden in East Sussex to learn from the best, and I couldn't help but put down roots in a country whose values felt so aligned with my own.

When a Chinese floral company caught wind of my work and asked if I would be willing to teach a series of workshops throughout China, off I went for a month of eating delicious dumplings and shopping the Shanghai flower market for treasures. I promised myself that if I could survive one month of translated classes in China (a daunting task to say the least), I could go to Japan afterward to restore my creative energy. A two-week trip to Kyoto became a two-month stay, which led to two years traveling back and forth to learn all I could about Japanese natural philosophy; it embraces grace and humility in a way I had never before experienced.

People often go far away to find themselves, but the more places I went, the more flowers I loved, and the more future selves I could imagine. I didn't find myself a home but instead found myself at home in the world.

No. 233

NATIONAL OPEN GARDEN SCHEME

YOU ARE WELCOME TO TRAVEL BY OUR PLANE

Mertensia Virginica

JAPAN
TOKYO

百合科 Liliaceae.

Fritillaria japonica, Miq.
こばいも　一名てんがいゆり

深圳航空 Shenzhen Airlines | A STAR ALLIANCE MEMBER ™

姓名 NAME MERRICK/AMYELIZABET

目的地 DEST. CHENGDU 成都
航班号 FLIGHT NO. CA 4338
日期 DATE 10OCT
座位号 SEAT NO. 62D
序号/舱位 BD NO./CLASS 208 / G

登机时间 BD TIME 1110
登机口 GATE 22
登机口可能变更请留意登机口 广播或登机口提示信息

N476096041

ETKD

9992386681457/1

Street-side sunshine in Romania.

Colors inspired by a California sunset: ranunculus, poppies, citrus, and lots of other treasures.

A sun hat and a sea of poppies at the Santa Barbara Botanic Garden.

Cacti wearing some very lovely hats.

A FLOWER

ARIZONA, USA

Vibrant, jewel-toned flowers
bursting from otherwise
barren cacti

CALIFORNIA, USA

Rolling mountains fluttering with
orange California poppies

CHINA

The motherland of roses, peonies,
and so many other garden flowers

EGYPT

Lotus, papyrus, and palms
carved into ancient stone reliefs,
with an oasis of verdant gardens
hugging the Nile

ENGLAND

Rose gardens, bluebell woods, and
drifts of hedgerow wildflowers

A flower adventure is an unfurling surprise.

ADVENTURE

JAPAN

Canopies of pink cherry blossoms
covering mossy green temples,
and ikebana classes to learn to
see more deeply

MOROCCO

Tiled paradise gardens of entrancing
jasmine, pomegranates, and citrus

ROMANIA

Cheerful flowers embroidered,
carved, and painted onto all sorts
of folk art

THAILAND

Wild orchids perched in jungle treetops,
and air plants dangling below

You never know precisely what you'll find when you step out the door.

THE WANDERLUST OF FLOWERS

When I started to travel in earnest, I didn't realize that flowers would be what held my hand along the way. Even when flowers weren't the basis of the trips, they became a familiar face in a crowd, my center of gravity when all else was moving. A rose in Paris is a rose in Morocco is a rose in the Chinese mountain village where it first bloomed as a wildflower thousands of years ago. And while the varieties shifted with each passport stamp, a thread of commonality wove its way through my travels. A dahlia that originated in Mexico could just as happily grow in a garden in England. And a tulip born in Turkey could flourish to acclaim in the Netherlands. Flowers don't care about borders; they know that the world is really just one place, after all.

I like to imagine the little bulbs hidden deep in saddlebags that were caravaned across continents by camels, or the minuscule seeds that were snugly wrapped in wax-paper envelopes and voyaged across the seas. Those original botanical explorers changed forever the course of nature, unifying far-flung domains in a single bouquet.

Opposite: In Japan, a poppy, with its eyes to the sky.

Above: Camellias in the rain in Kyoto.

Opposite: Camellias in a pool, visited by a matching snail.

Above: A native mullein, running wild at Great Dixter in East Sussex, England.

Opposite: The long border at Great Dixter is so much like a medieval tapestry that you'd almost expect to spot a unicorn in the garden.

FROM THE COMPOST PILE If you love gardens, there is no place on earth like England. I always imagined I'd make a horticultural pilgrimage there, but turning what could have been a simple tourist trip into something more substantial—a chance to learn to garden myself—was a dream I couldn't imagine until it came true. With a lot of luck and a little persistence, I was able to secure a three-month residency at Great Dixter, the most highly regarded of all English gardens. I worked, pinching and pruning, staking and potting, watering and weeding alongside some of the most gifted gardeners in the world. I fell in love with the nuances of nurturing a garden; it was an ever-changing arrangement that could envelop me entirely, not simply a small tableau to be admired only in a vase.

As a florist, I was an outlier from the start. Gardeners spend their days coaxing plants to reach their fullest potential, while florists march in with clippers, eager to cut them all down. During those months at Great Dixter, I suspended my eagerness to snip and instead learned to look for garden scraps everywhere, honing my eye for gems in what would have otherwise been compost. My little bedroom bloomed with a rotating assortment of cast-offs—a leaf, faded from green to yellow, in a vase, alongside a tall weedy grass destined for the garbage and a small pom-pom of hydrangea whose heavy head had snapped, looking almost as if it were made of porcelain when plucked off the ground. My inability to cut the beautiful flowers in the garden turned out to be a blessing, forcing my hand toward compost arranging: the art of appreciating the overlooked.

Opposite: My desk during my apprenticeship at Great Dixter, full of gardening books I read each night, dreaming of when I could plant a garden of my own.

An Englishman, his flower garden, and the little thatched cottage he built himself.

Rousham.

GARDENS
OPEN
10AM. LAST IN 4-30
TICKETS
FROM
MACHINE
£6-00p PER PERSON.
NO CHILDREN
UNDER 15.
NO DOGS.
NO PUSHCHAIRS.

An 'Angels' Choir' poppy.

Is there anything better
than spotting an arrangement
through a window?
Seen here at my friend
Charlotte's house.

Heaven is a handful of wildflowers.

GARDENS

FOR

FLOWER LOVERS

CHARLESTON FARMHOUSE
West Firle, East Sussex, UK

Flowers spring from every surface of the utterly charming Sussex home and garden of bohemian painters Vanessa Bell and Duncan Grant. The garden is a sweet jumble of roses and cottage flowers, and the house blooms with painted flower murals, woven floral rugs, and stenciled walls, lampshades, and curtain valances.

DUMBARTON OAKS
Washington, DC, USA

This historic estate, laid out in the 1920s by landscape architect Beatrix Farrand, shines with an elegantly proportioned series of terraced gardens, hedges, orchards, and tidy rows of flowers and vegetables; wild meadows and wooded walks await beyond the borders. The small orangerie is singularly divine, and so is the structure of the garden: the charming assortment of benches, gates, and outbuildings is beyond compare.

GREAT DIXTER
Northiam, East Sussex, UK

The wild, unruly plants that surround the fairy-tale Tudor manor house at Great Dixter weave an unrivaled patchwork of delight for the florally fascinated, making it a pilgrimage for passionate plantspeople from all over the world. Open for both casual visitors and keen students, Dixter is where my own adventure in English gardening began.

LONGWOOD GARDENS
Kennett Square, Pennsylvania, USA

Longwood Gardens quite nearly raised me as a little girl—my family would pilgrimage to this impressive botanical garden twice a year without fail. Its extensive series of Edwardian conservatories, year-round roses, orchid collection, and children's garden were my first-ever taste of what a garden could be. It captured my imagination and has held it firmly ever since.

LOTUSLAND
Montecito, California, USA

In this whimsical reverie of a garden, the use of desert and tropical plants sets a stage worthy of a classic silent film. Fittingly dramatic, as Lotusland was created by an opera singer with no background in horticulture whose Spanish Revival estate is one of the most fantastically personal, visionary gardens in America.

ROUSHAM
Rousham, Oxfordshire, UK

The idyll of the English countryside, Rousham is an eighteenth-century landscape garden designed by William Kent. Classical temples, follies, grottoes, and gently crumbling statues lull garden goers into a sense that time has not only stood still, it has ceased to exist at all. I recommend bringing a picnic to this delightfully relaxed haven, then sprawling on the lawn and pretending it is all yours for the day.

SISSINGHURST
Cranbrook, Kent, UK

Gardening grande dame Vita Sackville-West's rambling garden and estate hardly needs an introduction; it's one of the most beloved and famous gardens in England. A series of gracious and relaxedly formal hedged gardens sets the tone for feminine, lush plantings of cottage-garden flowers. Vita's towering library is a highlight, too, for its untouched collection of all her personal artifacts.

WAVE HILL
Bronx, New York, USA

In my New York days, Wave Hill was my sanctuary of happiness. The star of the property is its vista of the Hudson River, but the garden is beautiful down to the tiniest details; my favorite is the miniature alpine collection tucked into planters at the entrance of the delicately sized glasshouse. A free-spirited ethos and naturalistic plantings set the garden apart from the city outside.

Opposite: The very great Great Dixter garden in June, replete with hollyhocks, towering verbascum, and evening primrose.

A potted hellebore in an old tea container.

Vines, witch hazel, and evergreens in the tatami room where I first lived in Kyoto.

FINDING JAPAN

It's possible to be homesick for a place you've never been, somewhere you missed long before you ever arrived. I went to Japan to learn about flowers; of all my adventures, it was the most straightforward. I had been once before, but I had only explored Tokyo, a place of hustle and bustle: robots, heaving sidewalks, and trains that move so fast you can't even relax and enjoy the view. On this trip, I wanted to understand the natural philosophy of Japan and witness the part flowers play in their cultural heritage. I messaged a friend of a friend who lived in Kyoto—a woman named Kana Shimizu who had just opened a little jewel box of a café called Stardust in the northern reaches of the city. Housed in a nineteenth-century traditional *machiya*, with worn plaster walls cocooned in

an indigo patchwork of washi paper, the café radiated such warmth and spirit that I knew I had to start my trip there. I asked if she would be interested in having a small flower-arranging class together. Her response was a full-hearted yes, and she invited me to stay in the humble tatami room upstairs from the café.

Too afraid to take a taxi and face a comedy of mistranslations, I took the Kyoto public bus (the number 9 bus is the number 9 bus no matter the language). Stardust found me, really, and as I approached, I noticed the café's neighbor: an impossibly small but deeply elegant flower shop, complete with tatami mats, rustic Japanese ceramics, and numerous antique baskets full of unusual weedy wildflowers. It was nearly midnight by then, too late to cross that

magical threshold, but I could sense that even though I had never been there before, I was coming home.

I had thought I would complete my small workshop at Stardust, then stay for two weeks to explore, but instead I left two months later (and only after having purchased a plane ticket to return in another two months' time). Kana welcomed me completely into her world, and I was enchanted by her grace, peacefulness, and reverence for beauty down to the smallest detail. She introduced me to Hayato Nishiyama, the owner of Mitate, the flower shop next door, and to his philosophy of simple wildflower arranging—in the traditional tea ceremony style called *nageire*, derived from the flower arrangements created by Buddhist monks as temple offerings. Kana translated during a small class at the shop: four hours of discussing his philosophy of flowers, and then we picked a single leaf and a flower to place in a vase. The significance and respect given to a single stem reawakened my tenderness for flowers. Hayato had an illustrated book of Japanese flora and happily pointed to the wildflowers we'd chosen to arrange, and while we couldn't understand each other, we spoke the same language. His wife, Mica, made us matcha while their little three-year-old son, Man-chan, peeked out from behind a curtain. Hayato asked me one thing to end our class: When I went home, could I please share what I had learned about the spirit of Japanese wildflowers? Yes, I promised. I would.

Flowers for an autumn workshop at Stardust.

A cherry blossom party at Stardust in the spring.

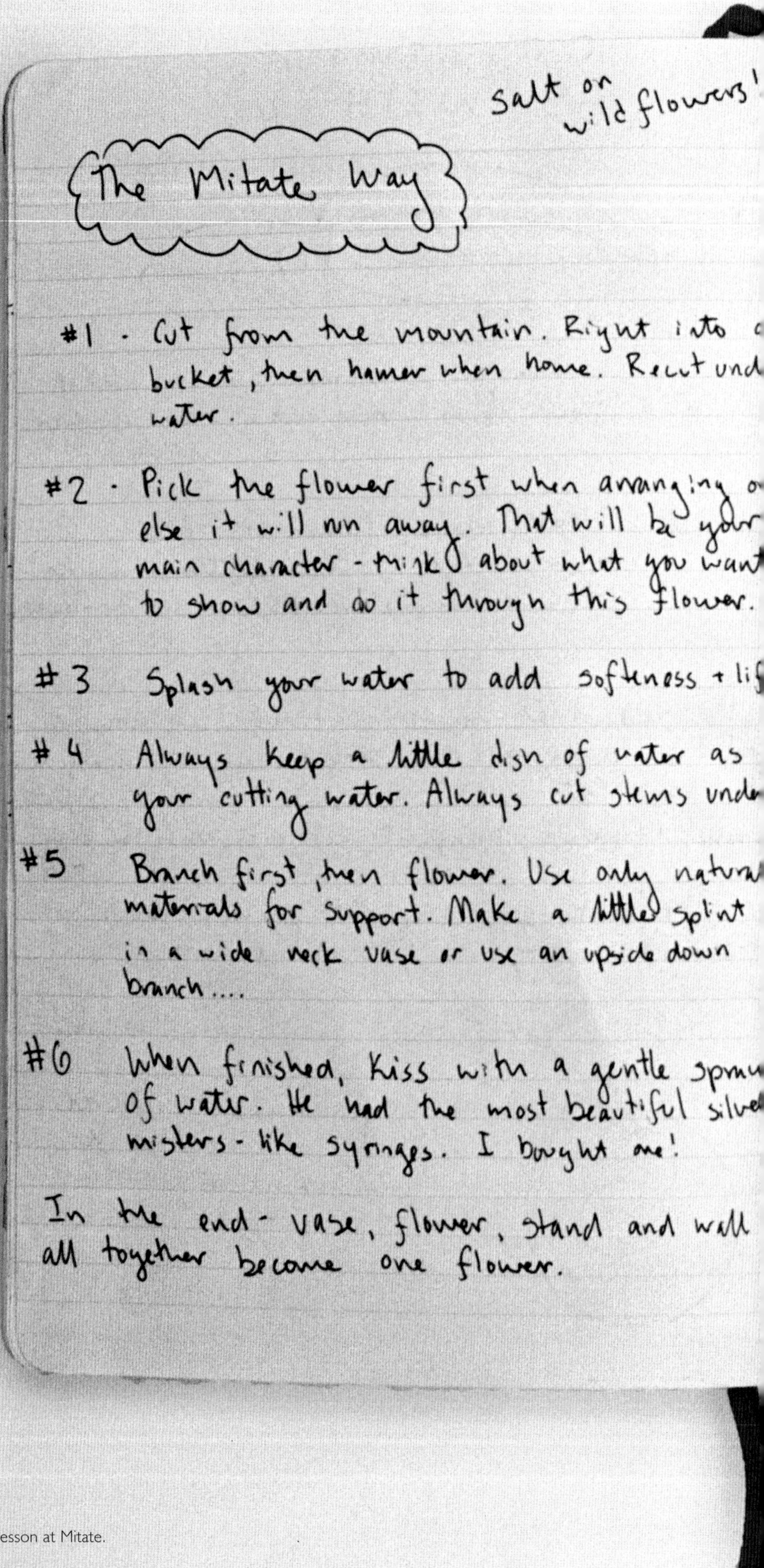

salt on
wild flowers!

{ The Mitate Way }

#1 · Cut from the mountain. Right into a
bucket, then hamer when home. Recut und
water.

#2 · Pick the flower first when arranging o
else it will run away. That will be your
main character - think about what you want
to show and do it through this flower.

#3   Splash your water to add softness + lif

#4   Always keep a little dish of water as
your cutting water. Always cut stems und

#5   Branch first, then flower. Use only natura
materials for support. Make a little splint
in a wide neck vase or use an upside down
branch....

#6   When finished, kiss with a gentle sprau
of water. He had the most beautiful silve
misters - like syringes. I bought one!

In the end - vase, flower, stand and wall
all together become one flower.

My travel journal, filled with notes from my lesson at Mitate.

Hikizan: stripping away excess to see true innocent beauty. Exposed, simple with nothing to hide.

Shimoyake: to be burned by heat or cold, Shimoyake ba. leaf burn

Mansaku: first bloom of the spring. (His son is named mansaku - man chan!)

☆ SEASONS IN IKEBANA

SPRING: Small buds unfurling + re-growth

SUMMER: SO HOT! Refreshing with exposed water.

FALL: HARVEST. Lots of Baskets, branches gathered, cold burned - not just seasonal red foliage.

WINTER: no flowers, bare, exposed camellia bud with perfect 3 leaves. The bud symbolizes all of the energy.

After we made our arrangements, he showed us in a wildflower book our choices! Mine was "Ligularia fissilaginea makino" a little yellow daisy everywhere in Japan in the fall. ♡♡♡

UNTRANSLATABLE JAPANESE WORDS ABOUT CHERRY BLOSSOMS

HANAFUBUKI

A moment of petals swirling in
the breeze; a blizzard of flowers

YOZAKURA

The experience of viewing
cherry trees at night

HANAIKADA

Clusters of flower petals drifting
together on black water

HANAZUKARE

The exhaustion one feels after a day
outdoors appreciating cherry blossoms

HANAAKARI

The subtle, pale glow of a cherry tree
when seen in the dark

WABIZAKURA

A solitary blooming cherry tree
with a sense of lonely beauty

Opposite: Sakuraame, a spring rain that washes
cherry petals off trees before they would fall naturally.

These are my clippers.

I travel with them everywhere (but never in a carry-on suitcase).

They're from a shop in Kyoto called Aritsugu

that's been forging blades since 1560.

The maker will carve your name into the handle,

but instead, I asked them to write the Japanese

character for home.

Now, no matter where I am, if I go to cut a flower,

home is in my hand.

Japanese wildflowers for sale at Mitate.

Mitate's collection of precious and beautiful vases.

BREAKING VASES

You should know straightaway that it was an accident, and honestly, my hands never even touched the vase in question. It almost seemed as if it had a will to break all on its own. I was living in a friend's graceful, traditional wooden house in an old neighborhood outside Osaka, studying ikebana and taking long weekends to explore the Japanese countryside. The house was a dream, built by his grandfather, with refined woodwork, whisper-thin shoji windows, hand-plastered walls, and a sunken kitchen with little seashells visible in the dust-pink earthen floor. I ate grilled oysters from the Sea of Japan right off the hibachi and drank sake from tiny ceramic cups, each wholly unique, speckled and crackled, priceless little treasures lined up on a shelf. I slept on a tatami mat, folding it up each morning in a ritual that even now has made me most comfortable sleeping on the floor. There was a cobalt-blue bathtub, deep enough for me to submerge myself in up to my ears, where in winter I soaked with dozens of bobbing yuzu to perfume the water and myself in turn. There was a small alcove in the wall made expressly to hold a flower arrangement to admire while you bathed.

Down a long hallway, delicate glass doors slid open to reveal a meticulously kept interior courtyard garden. A scarlet camellia pooled petals on the mossy ground; raised stone steps led windingly to a series of ancient stone lanterns. Along this glass wall was a cabinet holding special objects—glossy, colorful porcelain vases

and prehistoric bowls; mysterious artifacts I could not anchor in time or place. My friend said that I could use them to make arrangements whenever I liked. At the back of the cabinet, there was a small Chinese porcelain vase hand-painted with graceful, orange goldfish; I had some little speckled orange lilies that would be a perfect match. As I lifted the vase out of the cabinet, it brushed against the lip of a raggedy-looking pot sitting squarely in front of it. The contact felt infinitesimal, but the damage was not. The old gray pot's rim cracked right off, several large crumbling chunks falling to dust in the spotless cabinet.

Panic swept over me, then shock. I didn't know anything about the history of pot, only that it was clearly broken and I was clearly to blame. When my friend came home that evening, after an agony, I showed him the damage. He looked at me clear-eyed and told me that the vase was a thousand years old, and that it had been his father's favorite before he died. I then crumbled, too. He took a few moments, and then told me it was okay. The vase had had a long history before me, and I was now part of its story. With a sad smile, he said that all beautiful things in the world will break in the end. Looking back on that moment now, I can see that the vase was simply another fragment of beauty I would learn to piece together. Ephemeral and yet somehow eternal, like all the most enchanting things are.

FAR AWAY THINGS TO DO

Plan a pilgrimage to see a flower.

Throw a cherry blossom party.

Buy a one-way plane ticket.

Put flowers in your hotel room.

Collect vases as souvenirs.

Make peace with being lost.

Take a garden road trip.

Send postcards.

Bring thank-you cards (there is always someone to thank).

Keep a travel journal.

Notice flowers you've never seen.

Always opt for the window seat.

Appreciate homesickness.

Travel the globe in a single botanical garden.

Visit the city and spot nature all around.

Spend time in the country and see heaven in a wildflower.

Take simple joy in sumptuous pleasures.

Luxuriate in the smallest of things.

Go far away and feel at home.

Come home and see your world anew.

ACKNOWLEDGMENTS

The seeds of this book were planted by my family, without whom I would be entirely rootless. Thank you to my mom, Constance, whose free spirit infused my childhood with endless wonder, and to my dad, Tom, for sharing his love of plants from the beginning. To my sister, Micha, who carried buckets of flowers when I started my business; without you, I might still be glued to the sofa, paralyzed with fear at the thought of teaching my first class.

To Giulia Garbin, who patiently walked this path with me, page by page, to bring to life the design of the book. To Stephanie Madewell, whose gentle but deft word pruning and gracious encouragement over transatlantic phone calls kept me sane. To Miyuki Yamanaka, who drove me into the deep mountains of Nara for soba noodles and a soak in a hot spring, then gave me the courage to tackle the photography for the book on film. Her photos grace a handful of these pages, and from now on, I will always see the world through her lens.

Thank you to Artisan for the opportunity to be a part of your family, and especially to Lia Ronnen for her confidence in letting me create this book. To Bridget Monroe Itkin for skillfully crossing my *i*'s and dotting my *t*'s and providing thoughtful suggestions that were always sharper than even the sharpest red editor's pencil. To Michelle Ishay-Cohen for recognizing the love poured into these pages. To the rest of the Artisan team, including Sibylle Kazeroid, Nancy Murray, Jane Treuhaft, Hanh Le, and Elise Ramsbottom, for their unflagging patience and effort. To Kitty Cowles, who helped me stay the course. To Meghan Jablonski for the perspective. To Tif Hunter, F. Martin Ramin, Charlotte Bland, Adam Patrick Jones, Achim Kühn, and Alex Serrano.

To Siri, Margaret, and Joel Thorson for giving me a home on your farm and filling my arms with flowers. To Frances Palmer, who at the very beginning of my career stressed the importance

of frequent-flyer miles, and whose vases are truly a home for my flowers. To Alice Saunders for being the best kitchen table companion. To Kit Schultz, my Jo March, as I've turned out to be an Elinor Dashwood instead. To Anne Parker for the many methods she uses to make me coffee.

To Pedro da Costa Felgueiras, whose London home became my refuge and inspiration as I worked on this book. (I wrote in the garden room pictured on pages 150 and 151; it also appears on pages 36, 37, 132, and 152—all the elegant interiors!) To Tania and Jamie Compton for their open arms, from Spils to Braemar. To Charlotte and Donald Molesworth for showing me how thirty years of love can build a garden. To the people and plants of Great Dixter for letting me learn alongside you. To Claire Ptak of Violet Bakery for the cake. To Momo Mizutani of Momo-san, for loaning me your shop's shadows. To Charlie McCormick and Ben Pentreath for the chance to witness corgi puppies lapping double cream. And to Philip for the daisies, the dictionary, and actualizing page 39.

To Katagiri Atsunobu, who was sitting next to me when I received an email from Artisan asking if I was ready to create this book, and who implored me to find the courage to finally say yes. To Tok and Hiromi Kise for letting me use their glorious kitchen when I felt homesick, and to Tok for printing my book contract and reminding me, after seven rolls of destroyed film, that the true heart of this book was not merely in photographs. To Hayato and Mica Nishiyama, whose world at Mitate has forever changed how I see flowers. To Kana Shimizu, Rinn Suzuki, and the rest of my beautiful family at Stardust in Kyoto. And to the little table in the corner of Stardust where I signed the contract for this book, and to Kana Shimizu for then bringing me a celebratory glass of wine as I embarked on this journey. Now, with the deepest gratitude and tenderness, I raise one to all of you in return.